PRIORITIES FOR A
PLANET IN TRANSITION

THE SPACE BROTHERS' CASE
FOR JUSTICE AND FREEDOM

By the same author:

Online reference:

Our Elder Brothers Return – A History in Books
(1875 - Present)
published at www.biblioteca-ga.info

Books:

George Adamski – A Herald for the Space Brothers

Here to Help: UFOs and the Space Brothers

The author's books have also been
translated and published in
Dutch, Japanese, German and French.
Spanish translations are in progress.
Available from all major online vendors.

The author may be contacted at
info@bgapublications.nl

PRIORITIES FOR A PLANET IN TRANSITION

THE SPACE BROTHERS' CASE FOR JUSTICE AND FREEDOM

GERARD AARTSEN

Priorities for a Planet in Transition –
The Space Brothers' Case for Justice and Freedom
First published October 2015
(revised May 2017)

Photo credits:
Page vi: David D. Boyer. Page 13: Wang Xi Wen. Page 16: Simona Bocchi. Page 20 top: YouTube video still; bottom: NASA. Page 22: SOHO. Page 24: NASA. Page 40 top: Wendelle C. Stevens; bottom: YouTube video still. Page 41: Brit Elders. Page 54 top: photographer unknown; bottom: Robbert van den Broeke. Page 60: Ocean X; Hauke Vagt. Page 89: Harry Perton. Page 91: Per-Arne Mikalsen. Page 93: Mrs William Felton Barrett. Page 132: YouTube video stills. Page 150: Bernd Nachreiser.

ISBN-13/EAN-13: 978-90-815495-4-7

Published by BGA Publications, Amsterdam, the Netherlands
www.bgapublications.nl

Typeset in Calisto MT and Calibri

Cover design: Miguel Rubio

Cover photograph:
Video stills of unidentified flying object captured in BBC News coverage of mass protests in Hong Kong, 30 September 2014 (see p. 21 ff).

To humanity.

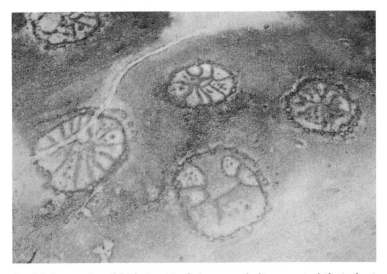

On 14 September 2011 the LiveScience website reported that giant wheel-shaped stone structures, such as pictured here in the Azraq Oasis, Jordan, had been discovered throughout the Middle East, which are believed to date back at least 2,000 years. According to information coming from Benjamin Creme (*Share International* magazine, November 2011) these are ancient records or drawings of spaceships. (Photo: © David D. Boyer)

Contents

List of photographs

Preface

More people than ever are dedicating their time to researching the UFO phenomenon – some by pursuing or investigating sightings, others by interviewing eyewitnesses, and others again by offering one theory after another. The UFOs themselves seem to be more willing to oblige than ever, with new sightings reported on a daily basis from around the globe, and although drones have recently entered the explain-away fray, ever fewer of these sightings can be dismissed by the usual debunking theories of swamp gas, weather balloons, satellites, lens flares and birds. And if they are top secret military craft, clearly the military should be firing those responsible for the many sightings despite their 'top secret' classification.

The presence of what can only be craft from other worlds is undeniable and well documented by eyewitness testimonies, photographs and video recordings and there is little if anything, therefore, that this book could add in that respect.

In my previous book, *Here to Help: UFOs and the Space Brothers*, I focused on uncovering the purpose of the extraterrestrial visits, based on the information coming from the initial contactees of the modern age from different parts of the world whose accounts and experiences were not contaminated by governmental or military disinformation. This resulted in a compelling account of how the efforts of the space people point to the interconnectedness of all life, including the planet and Cosmos, and how their message relates to humanity's own shared wisdom tradition.

We are presently finding out in every department of human life that we cannot continue to ignore the fact of our innate oneness with impunity – the crises that result from scorning this spiritual reality are piling up at an unprecedented rate. The number of assurances from economic observers or stock market analysts that return to economic growth is just around the corner – based on nothing more than the financial wizardry that has successfully been keeping up appearances of 'business as usual' – is now matched by the number of warnings of an impending collapse.

As has been foretold to many contactees, the fact that we have neglected the basic spiritual realities of life for millennia has brought us to the brink of global disaster. We have lived with greed and competition for so long that we have come to accept them as facts of nature. Many of us can't even imagine life without these twin assailants of human dignity, while the global elite happily feeds into this myth and successfully turns it into government policy in order to make a profit from every thinkable public service or human need.

Debunkers and detractors prefer to classify, or perhaps disparage, the messages from the early contactees as 'neo-religious'. However, in the context of the global crises, the current volume will show that they were in fact pathfinders or signposts to a renewed sense of our humanity, long overdue.

After addressing the question why the extraterrestrial visitors don't show themselves, this book presents yet more evidence that the information coming from many contactees, coinciding as it does with the Ageless Wisdom teaching, shows how their reports explain our cosmic isolation, showcase alternatives for the way we have organised society, and point the way ahead for humanity.

In addition, in each chapter a sidebar provides basic facts for concepts that readers may find unfamiliar or controversial and, likewise, for each chapter an addendum expands on an aspect with further background information which, it is hoped, will add to the reader's understanding.

Students of Ufology or the contactee era will find much that is confirmed and elucidated in world events and humanity's own wisdom traditions and, conversely, students of the Ageless Wisdom teachings will find these corroborated by the information coming from the Space Brothers.

Even in 1958 George Adamski said: "[T]oo much stress has been laid on the phenomena of sightings, and not enough on the advanced pathway of life these visitors have shown us. (...) It is my opinion, that were all groups to couple their research into sightings with a sincere study of the information given by the space people, the dissention [within the groups studying the flying saucers] would vanish and an expanding mode of living would open before them. For remember, the communications coming from the Brothers are not beautiful platitudes (...) but a liveable, workable, pattern for our daily lives."[1]

Priorities for a Planet in Transition – The Space Brothers' Case for Justice and Freedom will leave no doubt about the validity of this statement, because nearly sixty years on the "pattern for our daily lives" that is uncovered in these pages is more crucial for our survival than ever.

Amsterdam,
August 2015

---

1   George Adamski (1957-58), *Cosmic Science for the Promotion of Cosmic Principles and Truth*, Series No.1, Part No.3, Question #58

Acknowledgements
The author wishes to express his gratitude to all who granted permission to use their materials. He is also forever indebted to Benjamin Creme for his unremitting clarification of the Ageless Wisdom teachings.

1. The extraterrestrial presence: Seeing the forest for the trees

Seeing and hearing the public testimonies from a dozen or so officials confirming the extraterrestrial presence is a powerful statement of disclosure, as anyone will agree who has watched the recent 6-minute video compilation, titled 'Let's end the nonsense about UFOs and ET visitors'.[1] None of these testimonies were new – they had all been published separately over the span of the last six decades. Neither were they, so it seems, convincing enough for the mainstream media to give the subject the mature and thoughtful treatment it deserves. Seen together, though, an undeniable picture of positive disclosure emerges, coming from individuals who were or are active in the very realms of authority that are responsible for hiding the fact of the extraterrestrial presence from the public – government, science, and the military.

Most of these statements were also featured in my previous book, *Here to Help: UFOs and the Space Brothers*, showing how a growing number of officials are going on the record, such as FIDE President and former President of Kalmykia Kirsan Ilyumzhinov, Pope John XXIII, Apollo 14 astronaut Edgar Mitchell, Italian Consul Alberto Perego, Hungarian scientist Ervin László, former New Hampshire state legislator Henry McElroy Jr, former US Air Force Captain Robert Salas, and former Minister of Defence of Canada Paul T. Hellyer. Many more military and government officials could be added to this list, as well as an increasing number of celebrities, but since the publication of my book two further examples of dignitaries who speak out have come to my attention.

The first involves Lachezar Filipov, deputy director of the Bulgarian Space Research Institute, who stated in 2009: "Aliens are currently all around us, and are watching us all the time. They are not hostile towards us, rather, they want to help us but we have not grown enough in order to establish direct contact with them."[2] The Bulgarian scientific establishment felt embarrassed by the publicity that Mr Filipov's statements received and in good scientific tradition when it concerns the extraterrestrial presence on Earth, expressed their dismay at his open affiliation with the subject by stripping Mr Filipov of his positions. He, however, was not going to be silenced and in an interview on the Bulgarian BTV morning show *Tazi Sutrin* ('This Morning') in 2012 he confirmed: "I was pulled down from all positions that I had. My colleagues are embarrassed that I am concerned with and acknowledge the existence, and propagate the presence of an extraterrestrial intelligence."[3]

In the same interview he also describes a sighting of a UFO over Stalingrad (now Volgograd) in 1942 of which Joseph Stalin was informed, and Professor Filipov relates how his tutor heard the story from Soviet rocket engineer and space craft designer Sergei Korolyov. He continues: "In 1947 Stalin calls Korolyov and tells him, 'Take these four or five files', and locks him up in a room for three days to analyse the information that has been compiled about the UFO. After three days Korolyov comes out and says: 'This is exceptionally interesting technology. It does not pose any danger for us at the moment, but we know nothing about it.' From this moment on this file, all the documentation goes to the KGB."

In a further episode of the tacit and tangential disclosure that has been unfolding despite governments' best efforts, Russian Prime Minister and former President Dimitry Medvedev on 7 December 2012 made some comments to a reporter that seemingly should have remained off-air but made significant waves around the world when they found their way to the internet: "Along with the briefcase with the nuclear codes, the President of the country is given a special 'top secret' folder which is entirely devoted to the extraterrestrials who visited our planet. The report is provided by the special secret service which deals with the extraterrestrials in our country."[4]

If this is the file that Mr Korolyov was given access to in 1947, added to over the years we might assume, Russian presidents seem to have an advantage over their US counterparts, let alone the general public. Not for nothing did former Clinton chief of staff John Podesta express his regret over "once again not securing the disclosure of the UFO files" when he stepped down as advisor to President Barack Obama in February 2015. About the importance of official disclosure to the public Mr Podesta stated at a press conference organised by the Coalition for Freedom of Information in 2002: "It's time to find out what the truth really is that's out there. We ought to do it, really, because it's right. We ought to do it, quite frankly, because the American people can handle the truth. And we ought to do it because it's the law."[5]

As early as the late 1950s the Canadian engineer and government researcher Wilbert Smith stated: "We may ask, if all this is known, why has it not been publicized, why are not these matters being studied instead of atom bombs? The answer: it has been publicized." However, he adds, "Those who are in control of our society are satisfied with it the way it is and will resist any attempt to change anything which is likely to disturb the equanimity of their lives."[6] His observation was confirmed in comments by atmospheric physicist James E. McDonald, who openly criticised the policy that the US government instituted in the 1950s to make any release of information about UFOs at airbase level punishable with a fine of $10,000 or 10 years in prison, and "as a result of that nothing resembling any scientific investigation has been going on in the past 15 years".[7]

#5   In his *Cosmic Science* bulletin of June 1958, George Adamski reproduced parts of the Air Force Regulation 200-2 issued by then-Secretary of the Air Force Harold E. Talbott, dated 26 August 1953, which implied that all genuine UFO reports received by the Air Force must be kept from the public: "Information regarding a sighting may be released to the press or the general public by the Commander of the AF Base concerned only if it has been positively identified as a familiar or known object."[8]

Howard Menger, another of the early contactees, was also quite clear about the reasons for the silence of governments, even in 1959: "Government officials in particular refuse to tell because it would upset our economy. The knowledge they have gained depicts an entirely different way of life. It is living under God's law rather than man's law. Most mechanical energy sources would become obsolete."[9]

In the same vein as Wilbert Smith's question, many people who accept the extraterrestrial presence as a fact wonder "why they don't show themselves openly", "why they don't prove their existence by a mass landing", "why they remain so aloof", and similar ways of phrasing the same notion, which has been expressed from the beginning of the modern contactee era in the 1950s.

In response, George Adamski explained: "...without an understanding of who these people are, and their purpose in coming, their sudden appearance would indeed be terrifying."[10]

Who on Earth takes George Adamski seriously?

Based on his research, renowned UK author Timothy Good said that "many of Adamski's claims cannot be dismissed".[a] He also revealed that "Adamski held a US Government Ordnance Department identification card which gave him access to military bases, and he had regular meetings with military contacts who passed him sensitive information."[b]

After interviewing Adamski, science correspondent for the *Sunday Express* newspaper (UK) Robert Chapman said that "...if he were deluded he was the most lucid and intelligent deluded man I had ever met."[c]

About Adamski's much contested photographs J. Peverell Marley, a top Hollywood trick photographer at the time, stated that if faked, Adamski's pictures were the cleverest he had ever seen. And fourteen experts from leading British film company The Rank Group concluded that the object photographed was either real or a full-scale model.

Chief of the English Jetex Model Aircraft company Joseph Mansour said: "The reasons that I believe Adamski's photographs are not of models is that I think he himself is incapable of making a model sufficiently good from which these photographs could be faked."[d] And, if a full-scale model, it would have been "impossible without the expenditure of a large sum of money, and doubtfully even then, to make any model resemble the strange craft".[e]

Likewise, William Sherwood, an optical physicist at Eastman Kodak Company (USA), examined some of Adamski's later films of UFOs, and found them absolutely authentic.[f]

In his book *Alien Base* (1998) Timothy Good concludes: "Apart from my own prejudices, I feel it is important to re-emphasize that a great deal of what Adamski spoke and wrote about the 'space people' and their technologies is now, on the verge of the twenty-first century, more plausible and more scientifically relevant than it was some 40 years ago."[g]

Notes on page 36

He later added: "The visitors have made themselves incon-spicuous while on Earth, conforming rigidly to our customs; for they are aware many people still find it hard to believe advanced human beings surround us in space. They are cognizant of the ridicule those whom they contact must face..."[11] The Martian contact he called Firkon indeed said: "We do not enjoy the secrecy with which we have to make such meetings. We would far rather be welcome to come and go, and to visit with your people as we do with those of other worlds. But so long as our visits are not understood and are therefore made dangerous for us and our ships, we will have to continue with the present caution."[12]

Chilean author Enrique Barrios, who wrote about his 1985 experience in his novel *Ami, Child of the Stars*, was told that talking to individuals, as has been the space visitors' modus operandi, is "not interfering in the evolutionary development of the Earth. To show ourselves openly, to have mass communi-cation, would be"[13] and if there were to be a mass landing "thousands of people would die of shock. Remember all your movies about invaders? We are not inhumane, we wouldn't want to cause something like that."[14]

Howard Menger, too, said that the space people realize the danger of unintentionally destroying a lesser civilization by imposing their higher wisdom on those who cannot understand "and they are exercising great care in the manner of going about our education".[15] Adding elsewhere: "Mass landings, great displays, and the like would only cause confusion. The military would be involved immediately; the governments of the world would be in turmoil, each seeking its own advantage. There would be hysteria and, possibly, panic. And so, in the interest of humanity, the space people approach us cautiously."[16]

Benjamin Creme, the British esotericist who worked with

the space people in the 1950s, says: "They could land, make a big noise and tell us that they are here, but they do not. They make contact quietly, sensitively – so that they do not drive us to panic. If they come down and people panic and are terrified, the Space Brothers just go away. If the people are not terrified, if they do not panic, then things might happen."[17] As Menger's contacts told him: "We realize we cannot convince all the people of this world at one time; it might not be a good idea, anyhow; it might come as a great shock to people in low states of evolvement."[18]

Around 1965 Dutch contactee Stefan Denaerde was similarly informed that "[t]he cosmic isolation of an intelligent race can only be lifted when the minimum culture level has been reached; we call it 'social stability'."[19] Indeed, his contacts told him: "The most important thing for us is to ensure that your freedom of thought is not damaged. Freedom of thought is the essence of humanity, and if we were to damage that we would, according to our ethics, be committing a crime. Therefore, we will only convey knowledge to you, and not convictions."[20] So they urged him: "Write your book in clear science-fiction style and bring in certain inexactitudes, so that it cannot be used as irrefutable logic. You must leave people free to believe or not, as they choose. If anyone should ask you if it really happened, you must deny it and say that it is pure imagination. The people for whom the book is destined will say: 'I am not interested whether it really happened or not; for me, it is true. It has changed my insight and now I live consciously. I know the meaning behind life.' (…) *Never strive to be believed*. Your duty is only to publish this information and nothing more."[21]

It should not surprise us, then, that Adamski wrote, ten years prior: "All that they have asked of me is that I pass their knowledge on to my fellow man, whoever and wherever he may be. This I shall do, leaving to each man the privilege of believing or disbelieving, of benefiting from a higher knowledge, or casting it aside in derision and skepticism."[22]

As Wilbert Smith, himself a UFO researcher and contactee said, "There is a cosmic law against interfering in the affairs of others, so they are not allowed to help us directly even though they could easily do so. We must make our own choice of our own free will. Present trends indicate a series of events which may require the help of these people and they stand by ready and willing to render that help. In fact, they have already helped us a great deal, along lines which do not interfere with our freedom of choice."[23]

"The dividing line between help and interference is very delicate indeed and sometimes hard to perceive, but it is a mark of individual and collective progress how well we can be guided by it. (…) There is a basic law of the universe which grants each and every individual independence and freedom of choice, so that he may experience and learn from his experiences. No one has the right to interfere in the affairs of others. In fact, our Ten Commandments are directives against interference. If we disregard this law we must suffer the consequences, and a little thought will show that the present deplorable world state is directly attributable to violation of this principle."[24]

That the visitors from space take this 'prime directive' seriously also explains why they keep a low profile to the extent that many live and work among us without most people being aware of their presence. For instance, the visitors who contacted George Adamski told him: "We live and work here, because, as you know, it is necessary on Earth to earn money with which to buy clothing, food, and the many things that people must have. We have lived on your planet now for several years."

His Martian contact Firkon elaborated: "At our work and

in our leisure time we mingle with people here on Earth, never betraying the secret that we are inhabitants of other worlds. That would be dangerous, as you well know. We understand you people better than most of you know yourselves and can plainly see the reasons for many of the unhappy conditions that surround you."

"We are aware that you yourself have faced ridicule and criticism because of your persistence in proclaiming the reality of human life on other planets, which your scientists say are incapable of maintaining life. So you can well imagine what would happen to us if we so much as hinted that our *homes* are on other planets! If we stated the simple truth – that we have come to your Earth to work and to learn, just as some of you go to other nations to live and to study – we would be labeled insane.

"We are permitted to make brief visits to our home planets. Just as you long for a change of scene or to see old friends, so it is with us. It is necessary, of course, to arrange such absences during official holidays, or even over a week end, so that we will not be missed by our associates here on Earth."[25]

Howard Menger's contacts confirmed this: "[A] lot of our people are among you, mingling with you, observing and helping where they can. They are in all walks of life – working in factories, offices, banks. Some of them hold responsible positions in communities, in government. Some of them may be cleaning women, or even garbage collectors."[26] Therefore, as Benjamin Creme explains, if a space visitor "were an undisclosed worker for the Space Brothers, he would just appear as an ordinary man to you. You could not tell him apart as being or not being from another planet."[27]

In order to keep this low profile, they do ask for help from their contactees sometimes, as Menger elaborates: "I found I was actually helping them in little material ways, and such occasions

I enjoyed as much as the periods of instruction. Often I purchased clothing and took it to the points of contact. Visitors just arriving from other planets had to be attired in terrestrial clothing so they could pass unnoticed among people."[28] However, "[t]hey never asked me to obtain any identification papers for them or to help them locate jobs. They seemed to be able to take care of such matters themselves after they had been properly acclimatised and grown accustomed to our ways. Once clothed in our attire and briefed thoroughly in our customs, they were on their own, and seemed to experience no difficulties."[29]

George Adamski explains: "Let us remember that traveling space is not new to our neighbours. They have been coming our way for centuries, so family ties and friendships are well established throughout the world... Remember, too, that the necessity for personal identification papers is a comparatively recent requirement, particularly in the U.S.A... We have made much ado about personal identification papers, but actually, most of these are not too difficult to secure."[30] As documented in *Here to Help: UFOs and the Space Brothers*, very similar accounts have come forward about the Friendship Case of contact with well over a hundred Italians that started in 1956.[31]

Another American contactee, Buck Nelson, was also told there are many space visitors among us: "The folks I talked to spoke English very well. It seems that they learn the language of the people they will be contacting. They have told me that there are many of them amongst us. They have even taken some of our government officials up in their ships, but the officials are afraid to tell about it for they have too much to lose. I have no family to suffer for what might happen to me."[32] In blatant violation of the freedom of thought so strictly adhered to by the space visitors, and echoing the experiences of George Adamski, the Italian journalist Bruno Ghibaudi and many other contactees[33], Mr Nelson intimated: "I cannot say that I have been threatened, but I was offered a check for a thousand dollars if I would never tell my story again."[34]

The space people have always been well aware of the opposition faced by those that they contacted. As his contact Ramu told Adamski: "You are neither the first nor the only man on this world with whom we have talked. There are many others living in different parts of the Earth to whom we have come. Some who have dared to speak of their experiences have been persecuted – a few even unto what you call 'death'. Consequently, many have kept silent."[35]

In 1970, Dr James McDonald, who had criticized the US government for not taking the study of UFO sightings seriously, became a tragic example after he was deeply humiliated during a Congressional committee hearing where he gave evidence against the development of a supersonic transport plane, which could potentially harm the ozone layer. A congressman from a district where the plane would be built called his credibility into question by saying Dr McDonald believed in "little green men". His commitment to a scientific approach to the subject of UFOs had already led to marital problems, and when his wife wanted to divorce him after his public humiliation, he sadly decided to take his own life.[36]

So, while terrestrial authorities did everything in their power to prevent the public learning about the reality of extraterrestrial visitors, the people from space have always been careful not to force the reality of their existence upon the unprepared minds of people on Earth. However, they are far from shy to show their presence, and increasingly so in sightings that involve live audiences and TV cameras, as the following selection of recent sightings by media or other professionals shows.

On 17 July 2014 a Castanet crew was filming a report on the Smith Creek wildfire in West Kelowna, Canada. While interviewing the local fire chief, footage was shown of a firefighting airplane dropping its fire retardant load over the forest fire. From behind a cloud over the mountain in the background a bright circular object can be seen flying speedily across a patch of clear blue sky. In its online report about the sighting Castanet quotes the UFO Hunters website saying that since 2008 there have been 32 reported UFO sightings from Keremeos, British Columbia, near the US border to Salmon Arm, BC, 221 km to the north.[37]

On the morning of 10 February 2015 a production team of a Peruvian crime stopper show was filming in the Miraflores district of the capital Lima. The show is hosted by Renzo Reggiardo, who is also a congressman. The website *Peru This Week* writes: "Reggiardo had just begun filming for his programme *Alto al Crimen* when his camera man got distracted by something floating in the distant sky. They postponed filming a few moments to take a better look at the floating object." Others witnessed the strange craft as well and a member of the production team uploaded a video of the object on YouTube.[38]

In April 2014 an Australian crew were touring New Zealand and interviewing artists for Channel 74's *Colour In Your Life* art programme. On 3 April they were in Queenstown on the South Island filming the opening sequence for the show. While editing the episode a month later, the show's presenter Graeme Stevenson noticed two UFOs appearing from a wooded area in the background and speeding across the sky. No-one had spotted the objects during the filming, as they took just one second to cover a great distance.[39]

These are some random examples from around the world of sightings in fairly regional reports or programmes whose makers

On 23 August 2011 Wang Xin Wen, the CEO of a well-known Chinese shopping website, took some photographs from the Bund waterfront in Shanghai, China. In one of these she spotted a large UFO (circled) to the right of the famous television tower. She published both photographs on the Chinese Sina Weibo blogging website.

are just as stunned, sometimes after the fact, as live witnesses are when they see unearthly lights or actual craft in the skies, and similar reports could be added almost on a weekly basis. Of course, there are the inevitable hoaxes and publicity stunts, too, which debunkers gratefully welcome as proof that no one sighting should be taken seriously, such as the Space Centre's marketing stunt over the Nat Bailey Stadium in Vancouver, Canada on 9 September 2013[40] and the live news broadcast of the Argentinian news channel Todo Noticias on 28 February 2015, which caused quite a stir on the internet, but turned out to be fabricated when the news station posted the original broadcast on its website.[41] But in light of the examples above, such fabricated occurrences only serve to validate the reality of the ET presence given that there are those who feel the need to produce their own proof to the contrary.

One sighting that would certainly perplex even the hoaxers and debunkers today was that over Chicago O'Hare Airport's Gate C17 in November 2006 that was first reported by the *Chicago Tribune* newspaper on 1 January 2007.[42] Arguably the most memorable part of the reporting is an informal exchange between the *Tribune*'s Jon Hilkevitch, who wrote the report, and the host of the regional cable news network CLTV as they get ready for an interview. The exchange, which is available on YouTube, shows both mainstream newsmen sharing their excitement at the evidence that has come forward, including eyewitness statements from airport personnel and pilots.[43]

Likewise, in China in 2010 several UFO sightings, which were photographed by various people, made the news, some of which caused airport closures such as in Hangzhou, southwest of Shanghai, on 7 July that year and in Chongqing, 1700 km west of Shanghai, on 15 July.[44] On 20 August 2011 at 9pm a pilot on China Southern Airlines flight 6554 from Guangzhou to Shanghai saw a huge spacecraft. When he reported the situation to air traffic control he was told that they had already received reports from at least 10 other airplanes. This sighting, which was seen simultaneously over Shanghai and Beijing, was photographed as an expanding round white cloud.[45]

Of late, it seems ET craft are also not shy to show up for larger televised events. When US broadcaster NBC was reporting the evacuation of the Notre Dame University stadium in Notre Dame, Indiana on 3 September 2011, where a severe weather storm interrupted the match between the local Fighting Irish team and the visiting South Florida Bulls, one of the cameras was filming the sky when several bright white objects were seen shooting into a large, ominous looking cloud from which moments earlier lightning had shot out.[46]

Sightings over sports events have been reported as early as 1954, when spectators at the Stadio Artemi Franchi in Florence, Italy roared in excitement, not at the game but at several objects flying overhead, causing the referee to pause the game.[47] As with sightings in general, the attendance of off-world audiences seems to be on the increase, with similar sightings having been reported over London's Olympic Stadium towards the end of the opening ceremony's fireworks at 00:30am on July 27, 2012[48]; at the Weser Stadium in Bremen, Germany on 6 January 2014[49]; and the Nuevo Gasometro stadium in Bajo Flores, Argentina on 9 April 2014[50], for instance. (Interestingly, according to a report on the BBC London website, a UFO had already appeared over the Olympic Stadium in London while it was still under construction, in May 2009.[51])

Other much publicised events include a campaign speech by then Democratic presidential candidate Barack Obama, in Pueblo, Colorado, USA on 1 November 2008, three days

UFO photographed over the Maha Kumbh Mela in Allahabad, India on 9 February 2013. (Photo: © Simona Bocchi)

before his election. The UFO was spotted by someone who saw the MSNBC footage of the speech. On 20 January 2009, about 30 minutes before the start of president-elect Obama's inauguration in Washington DC, a CNN camera was filming the crowds that had gathered for the event, when an object that looked like a disk flew past the Washington Monument and over the crowd before flying out of view.[52]

One mass event that was observed by a UFO was the 2013 Maha Kumbh Mela, the largest gathering of Hindu faithful in the world that is held once every three years in one of four cities in India. From 14 January to 10 March 2013 an estimated 100 million people were expected to visit the *sangam* (confluence) of the sacred Ganges and Yamuna rivers in Allahabad for a ritual bath. On 9 February, when an estimated eight million people had gathered on the rivers' banks, Simona Bocchi, a renowned Italian artist living in India, was in Allahabad and took some photographs of the sky over the confluence. Upon inspection, one of her photographs showed a space craft that was not visible to the naked eye. Mrs Bocchi has long thought that extraterrestrial life exists and in recent years began to experience sightings which she sometimes depicts in her art.

Through his telepathic contact and work with a Master of Wisdom, one of humanity's Elder Brothers who he says are returning into the everyday world at this time to oversee our safe transition into a new age of justice and freedom for all, Benjamin Creme regularly confirms the sightings of extraterrestrial craft in *Share International* magazine, of which he is the chief editor, often adding where the space ship that was sighted originated from. In the case of Mrs Bocchi's photo, however, Mr Creme's Master volunteered some further information: "The occupants of the spacecraft were photographing the Mela. People in Mars are very interested in what goes on on

Earth and they do not all travel in spacecraft. Some are brought here to show them, however."[53]

To many who are not familiar with this kind of telepathic rapport between a Master of Wisdom and one of his working disciples in the everyday world, this might seem far-fetched, but to anyone who is familiar with the experiences of the early contactees the notion of interplanetary tourism is not at all a foreign one. For instance, on his first visit to a mothership George Adamski is told by Kalna, one of his hosts from Venus: "Many such ships have been built, not only on Venus, but also on Mars and Saturn and many other planets. However, they are not intended for the exclusive use of any particular planet, but for the purpose of contributing to the education and pleasure of all citizens in the whole brotherhood of the Universe. People naturally are great explorers. Therefore, travel in our worlds is not the privilege of the few, but of all. Every three months a fourth of the inhabitants of our planets embark on these gigantic ships and set out for a cruise through space, stopping at other planets just as your cruise liners stop at foreign ports. In this way our people learn about the mighty Universe and are enabled to see, firsthand, a little more of the 'many mansions' in the Father's house to which your Bible refers."[54]

In answer to a question Adamski later added: "Inherently, man is a traveler. He enjoys visiting new places, seeing new sights, and meeting new people. The fortunate ones in our world who are able to spend months or years in other countries learning their languages, their customs, and receiving new ideas from the people with whom they come in contact, gain much knowledge in this way alone. (...) It is regrettable that our monetary system makes it impossible for the vast majority of Earth's people to enjoy extensive travel."[55] However, on the other planets, according to Stefan Denaerde's contacts, "we have no money, but

18

everyone can go on holiday in this way if they wish."[56]

Adamski added that it will also become possible for Earthlings to be picked up by a space ship and taken to another planet for a vacation to learn more about their way of life. "I believe this time will come when excursions like this will be more than a possibility. However, so long as we remain hostile to those coming from outer space, or continue to react with intense fear when their ships come close, such vacation trips are not feasible."[57]

Several contactees have said how much their space contacts appreciate the beauty of our planet. The Italian contactee Giorgio Dibitonto was told on his first meeting with Raphael (or Ramu, as Adamski called him): "How beautiful it is! ... Your Earth is one of the most beautiful in the cosmos. But, in spite of that, it is in danger, because of the pride and egotism of those who would risk a destruction of unimaginable proportions. Since earliest times, we have endeavoured to help you, to prevent the catastrophe that you are now preparing for the Earth, and to influence you and your actions for the good. However, we can only do that in a way that provides for your own development with complete freedom. Among us there is no desire to use force over other people; we do not lust for power."[58] On a subsequent contact, Raphael talked about Earth as "one of the most beautiful dwelling places in the universal Father's kingdom".[59] Similarly, Dutch contactee Stefan Denaerde was told: "This is the blue planet with the blinding light, the home of the graceful, long-legged human race. It is one of the most beautiful planets that we know..."[60]

Less formal events of a political nature, although perhaps more significant in terms of the changes necessary in today's world, are also receiving their share of the space visitors' attention. At the end of a march in Berlin, Germany on 12 November

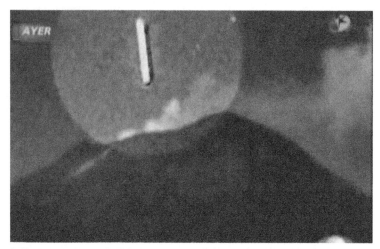

Cylindrical-shaped objects caught flying into the mouth of Mount Popocatépetl, Mexico on 25 October 2012 (above) and photographed over the surface of Mars on 28 April 2014 (below).

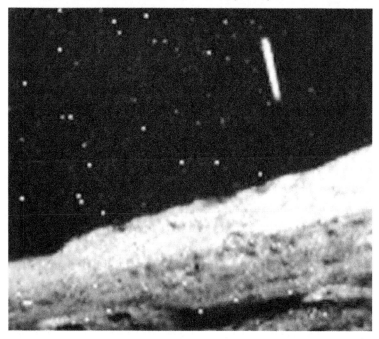

2012, a UFO was sighted over the Brandenburger Gate by some of the demonstrators, as the crowd was about to be addressed from the stage.[61] And during the massive protests in Brazil in June 2013 a UFO was filmed over the crowds protesting in Largo da Batata, in downtown Sao Paolo, appearing as a glowing ball of light. The demonstrations started in April that year to protest increases in public transport fares in some Brazilian cities, but came to include other social issues as the rallies continued. The UFO that was seen on 17 June, as reported by the *International Business Times* of 20 June, was soon discarded as a drone by many, in good debunker's fashion, even though several UFO websites showed videos of drones, that were clearly recognisable as such, alongside the video of the UFO.[62]

In a commentary on the Brazilian protests sighting Collective Evolution editor Arjun Walia writes: "This is something planet Earth has never seen before. The people are waking up and standing up to what no longer resonates with them on a mass scale. Right now, mass protests are happening in Brazil, to name one place. People coming together is what it's all about.

"In the end it is our choice which direction we choose to go. Either move forward, grow and thrive from a place of love, peace, co-operation and understanding, or not. If we choose the first, maybe we will continue to attract friends in 'high places' that feel the same way... We are not alone. Maybe some others out there want to see us change the world, and live in a more harmonious way with each other, the planet and all of the beings that reside upon it."

"The UFO phenomenon [...] seems to be coinciding with this mass awakening that's taking place. UFO sighting reports continue to increase exponentially every month as the consciousness of the human race continues to expand and grow."[63]

When Vincent Smith of Blantyre, Scotland was watching

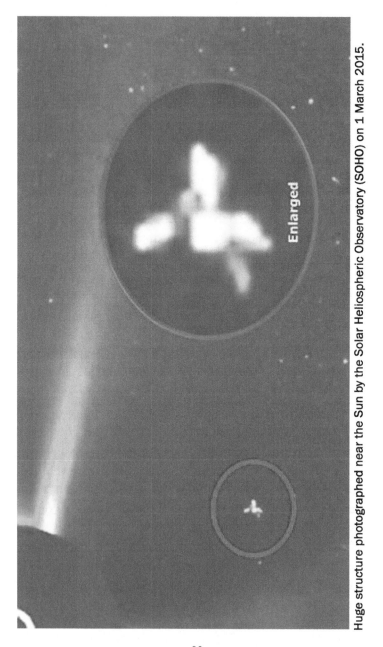

Enlarged

Huge structure photographed near the Sun by the Solar Heliospheric Observatory (SOHO) on 1 March 2015.

the live BBC coverage of the pro-democracy protests in Hong Kong on 30 September 2014, he suddenly noticed a bright greenish object flying across the sky in the distance. The object could be seen flying between buildings from left to right, descending slowly and when it was above a building to the right of the screen it took off vertically. Again, debunkers wasted no time to explain it was a drone, but both the light of the object and the speed with which it took off would require drone technology which is not of this Earth.[64]

Even if some sightings are of media drones, there are plenty of sightings which will not be so easily explained away, such as the one kilometre long cylindrical UFO seen entering the mouth of Mount Popocatépetl, an active volcano south-east of Mexico City, as recorded by a fixed camera for Televisa, a major Mexican TV network, after a sudden eruption on 25 October 2012[65], and another that was recorded by the same camera on 30 May 2013, or else the UFO that was seen destroying a meteor over Russia on 15 February 2013.[66]

Those interested in the UFO phenomenon will know that sightings are not limited to Earth either. While unusual sightings from or around the International Space Station[67] could be and usually are explained, or explained away, as artefacts or space debris[68], that explanation would not hold water for the cylindrical craft photographed on Mars on 28 April 2014 by the Curiosity rover[69], similar in shape to that seen entering Popocatépetl in October 2012. Other recent off-Earth sightings involve a flying object that appeared in a rover photograph that was taken on 14 July 2014[70], bright lights on Mars on 3 April 2014[71] and on Ceres, the largest object in the asteroid belt between Mars and Jupiter, on 19 February 2015[72], and a huge structure photographed near the Sun by the Solar Heliospheric Observatory (SOHO) on 1 March 2015.[73]

Bright lights were photographed on Mars on 3 April 2014 by Mars rover Curiosity (above), and on Ceres, the largest object in the asteroid belt between Mars and Jupiter, on 19 February 2015 (below) and 6 June 2015 (inset) by the Dawn space probe. (Photographs: NASA)

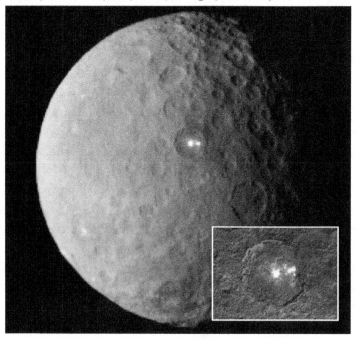

As with the statements from officials disclosing the extra-terrestrial presence on Earth, the fact that this chapter describes two dozen or so sightings by media and other professionals over the span of just a few years that mostly allow no room for debate about their authenticity leaves one to wonder how long the media as a whole would maintain their trademark dismissiveness if they were to see the 'news' that presents itself in the bigger picture which they overlook in their hunt for daily headlines?

Readers with an understanding of how our thoughts, emotions and daily lives are interconnected will see a definite reciprocal relationship here: as long as, individually, we are ever poised to run after the next spectacle, be it to hail or to debunk it, often not even allowing ourselves the time to establish the details, let alone to savour the experience, we ourselves are not allowing the bigger picture to form on the basis of authentic sightings and their facts. If the media represent a magnification of our interests and desires and so will give us the instant satisfaction we long for, if we ourselves are too distracted by the trees to see the forest, we cannot blame only the media for providing us with spectacle instead of substance.

In any case, it should now be clear that there is no truth to the notion that 'they' don't show themselves – quite the contrary. The inevitable conclusion is that they do show themselves, that they do so not just around the world but increasingly around the solar system, and that they are seeking our attention. As always though, they do so without infringing our freedom of thought and with respect for our right to deny the obvious.

Chapter 1 Addendum:
'Out of the mouth of babes...'

In his book *The Gathering of the Forces of Light – UFOs and their Spiritual Mission* (2010), Benjamin Creme says about contactees being ridiculed: "We ridicule those who tell the truth [about the ET presence], even when we recognize it as such. We tend to reject the truth because it means a change in oneself, in one's way of thinking, feeling, acting and reacting. It means a real psychological change, so it is difficult. It is easier, therefore, to deny than to affirm."[74]

So prevalent is this ridicule, and indeed people's fear of being ridiculed, that we often deny that which we saw with our own eyes. In the same book Mr Creme describes a stunning example of this when he and his wife were in north Wales with a friend who said she would love to see a flying saucer. "Would you believe it if you saw it?" he asks his friend, who replies: "Yes, I would believe it. If I could see it with my own eyes, of course I would believe it." When indeed a spectacular sighting takes place within a second, the friend shouted: "I have seen a flying saucer! I have seen a flying saucer! Well, at least Ben said it was a saucer. But it couldn't have been. It just could not have been a saucer. No, it could not have been. No."[75] Such is the power of the conditioning that we allow ourselves to be subjected to.

Children, by contrast, are not yet conditioned by what is considered 'acceptable' or not and are much more open to the unusual, even beyond the 'magic' years of early childhood. So when one girl came home telling her parents she had seen a UFO she was told not to talk about it and that she had imagined it all. Except she was one of 62 (!) children at the Ariel School in Ruwa, Zimbabwe who witnessed this sighting just outside the school's playground on 16 September 1994.[76] Shortly after the event several of the children, who were between 6 and 12 years old, were interviewed by Zimbabwean UFO researcher Cynthia Hind and BBC reporter Tim Leach, who found that although the children's stories differed in their description of the craft, overall they were remarkably consistent, which convinced the staff that the students had seen something very unusual.

Some of the children who were closest to the landing site reported seeing small beings of about 1 metre tall with large heads and wearing shiny one-piece suits.[77] Some said they had been frightened because of the way the beings from the craft stared at them. When Harvard psychology professor John Mack interviewed some of the children a few months later he asked, "Why do you think they want us to be scared?" one girl replied, "Maybe because we don't look after the planet and the air properly."[78] In fact, several of the students said they 'felt' like they were here to warn us about the dangers of pollution. In an interview with Dutch TV personality Tineke de Nooij, several of the children said they felt privileged to have witnessed the ET visit, with one girl saying: "I think they want people to know that we're actually making harm on this world and we mustn't get too technologed."[79]

Reports in *Flying Saucer Review* going back to the 1950s, and especially in *UFO AfriNews*, the publication that Cynthia Hind edited from 1988 until her passing in 2000, show that many more sightings have taken place across the African continent, which the rest of the world is often not aware of because the majority of researchers, who are mostly located elsewhere, are concerned with sightings and debunkers in their own country or continent. Fortunately, though, Mrs Hind has researched and documented various cases that occurred on the African continent in her books UFOs – African Encounters and UFOs over Africa.

One of these involved four young school boys aged 12 to 16 years old who saw 3 'silver men' on a hill in Groendal Wilderness Reserve near Uitenhage in Eastern Cape, South Africa. Although they stated that they hadn't previously read any books or seen films about UFOs, their close encounter left them puzzled to such an extent that they feared ridicule if they would tell the authorities.

On Monday 2 October 1978, after a night camping out in the wilderness, Peter Simpson, 16, Jannie Bezuidenhout, 15, Hugo

Ferreira, 12, and Joe Perino, 13, from nearby Despatch were waiting to be picked up by Peter's mother at 11:15am. While seated on the ground, waiting for their lift, Peter says, "We all four of us saw this silver thing glisten between the trees on the side opposite to us and about 900 metres away. I thought it was a large stone shining in the sun…" At the same time Jannie Bezuidenhout saw two silver men at about 275 metres from where the boys were. Peter says they first thought the men were poachers. "But then we could see they wore silver suits like fire-fighters. (…) There were two men at first and they were moving in a strange way. They didn't have any noticeable walking movement, it looked more as thought they were gliding over the surface." Hugo Ferreira adds: "I thought their silver suits looked just like aluminium foil." Both Hugo and Joe agreed that the men appeared to be moving on trolleys.

Peter says: "The two men came from the direction of the glistening object. When they were in the middle of the hill, they were joined by a third man who was carrying a silver square suitcase. I don't know where the third man came from; he just suddenly appeared."

The boys saw the men, who appeared to be of adult human size, climb over a fence when one of them looked in the boys' direction. "It seemed as though he stopped, waiting for the other two to go through the fence and then he looked at us. I could see then that the silver suit he wore came down over his forehead and then where his face was, that was grey." According to Peter the men then "went along the fence towards the top of the hill and they then disappeared." Asked if they went over the top of the hill, he replied: "No they just suddenly disappeared." Hugo Ferreira added that when the men disappeared, the 'round thing' was also gone.

Peter Simpson also noticed that as the men walked up the fairly steep hill, they did not bend forward as people would normally do, but stayed upright instead. He also thought that a fit man would take at least 10 minutes to get up that hill, whereas the entire sighting, according to the boys, did not last more than

50 to 60 seconds. Upon investigation by Weekend Post reporter Keith Ross, a police officer, two trackers, and a photographer, it turned out that the area where the strange men were seen was not grassed over, as it seemed from a distance, but covered in fynbos or shrub over 2 metres high and almost inaccessible. It took the party one-and-a-half hours to reach the spot, where they also found a "fairly large depressed site". According to police major Chris Powell, "the depression was not formed by anything normal. The marks were too symmetrical."

Instead of waiting at the agreed pick-up spot, the boys excitedly went over to the warden's house, but didn't tell him about it for fear of being laughed at. When Peter's mother suggested they tell Mr Zeelie, her son objected: "Please Mom, he's going to laugh at us, this is too far-fetched."[80]

The Ruwa and Uitenhage episodes certainly weren't the only or the first sightings of extraterrestrial craft or beings by children. On 6 April 1966 hundreds of students and teachers at Westall High School and local residents of the Westall suburb of Melbourne, Australia witnessed a UFO hover overhead for several minutes before it took off at incredible speed. While the incident had drawn the attention of the Channel 9 television network and a local newspaper, a 2010 documentary shows that the students were not only disbelieved by many adults, but even silenced by the authorities, with the headmaster asserting to the students they had not seen a flying saucer. He told them they had not seen anything and they were not to talk to anybody about... well, not seeing anything.[81]

Also in 1966, early March, two children in Carson City, Michigan, USA witnessed a spacecraft that had landed in a small enclosed field at the edge of town. Then 7 years old, the witness who reported the sighting to the Mutual UFO Network states that she and her cousin saw a disc-shaped craft ascend in a zigzag manner from among scattered pieces of metal lying around. When the mother went back to the field she found a flattened burnt area where the children first spotted the disc.[82] And on 29 August 1967, François and Anne-Marie Delpeuch, 13 and 9 years old, respectively, were out with their dog in the field near the small village of Cussac, France, where they lived, when they saw what seemed to be four children and a large sphere behind a hedge, some 40 metres away. The sphere of about 2 metres in diameter was so brilliant that it hurt their eyes. When François called over to ask if the 'children' had come to play with him and his sister, they abandoned what they were doing and rushed to board the sphere and took off. According to the children the little beings were about 1 metre to 1.20 metres tall and were clad in tight fitting shiny black suits.[83]

Compared to the eyewitnesses in Westall, the children in the latter two cases were fortunate to be taken seriously, with several media and researchers visiting to investigate their story. After reading my previous book Dutch film maker Falco Friedhoff wanted to meet me to share his story of a close encounter with a flying saucer and its occupant when he was a child.

In 1952, at a time when Holland was still suffering from a severe housing shortage as a result of World War II, the Friedhoff family was one of five families housed in a large stately home in the wealthy Dutch town of Bloemendaal which before the war was owned by the governor of the Dutch Central Bank.

Falco Friedhoff was 4 years old and playing with his toy cars that he drove on the roads and in the tunnels that he had built in the sand. It was a sunny day and that afternoon, against a sheer blue sky, all of a sudden he saw a flying saucer, hovering at a distance of about 20 metres away from him. The saucer was small and had a tall glass dome.

As the saucer hung still, the pilot was clearly visible. To the best of his memory, based on the distance between himself and the saucer, Mr Friedhoff estimates that the man in the saucer would have measured around 1 metre standing. Speaking about the experience 60-odd years on, he says: "It's as clear in my memory as if it happened yesterday. And as a 4-year-old it just seemed the most normal thing in the world. I was completely unperturbed at the sight of a flying saucer with a small man inside. I waved at him. I don't remember if he waved back or just smiled, but he did acknowledge me in a friendly manner. We had eye contact."[84]

Although the saucer looked exactly like the type Mr Friedhoff would later see in some comic strips or popular illustrations, he is adamant that he didn't see those until years later. Just as he never saw the saucer coming, Mr Friedhoff says the saucer disappeared without him seeing it fly away.

These accounts serve to show us how much richer our lives would be, and more in touch with reality, if we could see the world through mature eyes with the innocence of childhood intact.

Notes

1 Gerard Aartsen (2015), 'End the UFO/ET disclosure nonsense!'. Available at <www.youtube.com/watch?v=U78n64c8K7A>
2 'Aliens "already exist on earth", Bulgarian scientists claim', *The Telegraph* [online], 26 November 2009. Available at <www.telegraph.co.uk/news/worldnews/europe/bulgaria/6650677/Aliens-already-exist-on-earth-Bulgarian-scientists-claim.html> [Accessed 2 March 2015]
3 Interview with Lachezar Filipov on BTV, Bulgaria, October 2012. Available at <www. youtube.com/watch?v=23WRbbWFBQI> [Accessed 2 March 2015]
4 Off-air comments made after an interview on Russian TV, 7 December 2012. Available at <www.youtube.com/watch?v=fnpmjXhQT9w>
5 Andrew Buncombe (2015), 'US Presidential aide John Podesta says biggest regret is not securing release of government records about UFOs'. *The Independent* [online], 16 February. Available at <www.independent.co.uk/news/world/americas/us-presidential-aide-john-podesta-says-biggest-regret-is-not-securing-release-of-government-records-about-ufos-10049486.html> [Accessed 2 March 2015]
6 Wilbert Smith (1969), *The Boys from Topside*, p.28
7 Interview with James McDonald (archival footage), in: Rosie Jones (dir.; 2010), *Westall '66: A Suburban UFO Mystery*. Screen Australia, Film Victoria, Endangered Pictures, Australia. Available at <www.youtube.com/playlist?list= PL6499D07FE5268266>
8 George Adamski (1957-58), *Cosmic Science for the Promotion of Cosmic Principles and Truths – Questions and Answers*, Series No. 1, Part No.4
9 Howard Menger (1959), *From Outer Space to You*, pp.163-64
10 George Adamski (1957-58), op cit, Part No. 1, Question #17
11 Ibidem, Part 3, Question #57

12 Adamski (1955), *Inside the Space Ships*, p.176
13 Enrique Barrios (1989), *Ami, Child of the Stars*, p.32
14 Ibid., p.26
15 Menger (1959), op cit, p.108
16 Ibid., p.161
17 Benjamin Creme (2010), *The Gathering of the Forces of Light – UFOs and their Spiritual Mission*, p.16
18 Menger (1959), op cit, p.75
19 Stefan Denaerde (1977), *Operation Survival Earth*, p.16
20 Ibid., p.25
21 Ibid., p.153
22 Adamski (1955), op cit, pp.126-27
23 Smith (1969), op cit, p.29
24 Ibid., p.17
25 Adamski (1955), op cit, pp. 38-39
26 Menger (1959), op cit, p.92
27 Creme (2010), op cit, p.41
28 Menger (1959), op cit, p.71
29 Ibid., p.73
30 Adamski (1957-58), op cit, Part No.5, Question #97
31 See Stefano Breccia (2009), *Mass Contact*, p.153 ff
32 Buck Nelson (1956), *My Trip to Mars, the Moon, and Venus*, p.13
33 See e.g. Gerard Aartsen (2011), *Here to Help: UFOs and the Space Brothers*, 2nd edition 2012, pp.18-19 and 20-21 for some examples of attempts to intimidate contactees out of sharing their experiences.
34 Nelson (1956), op cit, p.13
35 Adamski (1955), op cit. p.40
36 Wikipedia entry on James E. McDonald. Available at <en.wikipedia.org/wiki/James_E._McDonald#Late_life_and_death> [Accessed 29 March 2015)
37 'Castanet's UFO? Video'. Castanet website, 13 August 2014. Available at: <www.castanet.net/news/West-Kelowna/120861/Castanet-s-UFO-video> [Accessed 7 March 2015]
38 Hillary Ojeda (2015), 'YouTube: Unidentified flying object recorded in Lima today'. *Peru This Week* [online], 11 February. Available at <www.peruthisweek.com/news-youtube-this-could-actually-be-ufo-filmed-in-lima-105252> [Accessed 7 March 2015]
39 Sophie Ryan (2014), 'UFOs captured on film near Queenstown'. *The New Zealand Herald* [online], 14 May. Available at <www.nzherald.co.nz/nz/news/article.cfm?c_id=1&objectid=11254875> [Accessed 7 March 2015]
40 Megan Stewart (2013), 'Nat Baily UFO now identified as Space Centre "hoax"'. *Vancouver Courier* [online], 10 September. Available at <www.

vancourier.com/sports/nat-bailey-ufo-now-identified-as-space-centre-hoax-1.618998> [Accessed 7 March 2015]

41 'Viralísimo: el mundo habla de un "ovni" que apareció al aire en TN'. Todas Noticias [online], 6 March 2015. Available at <tn.com.ar/tecno/f5/viralisimo-el-mundo-habla-de-un-ovni-que-aparecio-al-aire-en-tn_575204> [Accessed 7 March 2015]

42 Jon Hilkevitch (2007), 'In the sky! A bird? A plane? A ... UFO?'. *Chicago Tribune* [online], January 7. Available at <articles.chicagotribune.com/2007-01-01/travel/chi-0701010141jan01_1_craig-burzych-controllers-in-o-hare-tower-united-plane> [Accessed 10 March 2015]

43 'UFO Over Chicago O'Hare'. CrypticMedia [online], 30 August 2007. Available at <youtu.be/0HUte_H9LKY> [Accessed 10 March 2015]

44 'Second UFO seen over Chongqing'. China.org.cn [online], 16 July 2010. Available at <www.china.org.cn/china/2010-07/16/content_20509901.htm> [Accessed 10 March 2015]

45 'Mystery of glowing white ball in the sky'. English Eastday, 23 August 2011. Available at <english.eastday.com/e/110823/u1a6067786.html> [Accessed 10 March 2015]

46 John Stevens (2011), ' "UFOs" spotted over football stadium as Notre Dame game comes to a standstill'. Mail Online, 9 September. Available at <www.dailymail.co.uk/news/article-2035758/UFOs-spotted-football-stadium-game-comes-standstill.html> [Accessed 7 March 2015]

47 Richard Padula (2014), 'The day UFOs stopped play'. BBC News [online], 24 October. Available at <m.bbc.com/news/magazine-29342407> [Accessed 7 March 2015]

48 Natalie Evans (2012), 'UF-Olympics? "Alien spacecraft" caught on camera over the London 2012 opening ceremony'. *Daily Mirror* [online], 31 July. Available at <www.mirror.co.uk/news/uk-news/ufo-spotted-at-olympic-games-opening-1193663>. [Accessed 10 March 2015] Benjamin Creme's Master confirmed that this craft did not belong to the Space Brothers, but that it was the lightship used by humanity's Eldest Brother, World Teacher Maitreya (see *Share International* magazine, Vol. 31, No.7, p.13).

49 'Es leuchtete und schwebte über das Weserstadion'. Der Bund [online], 9 January 2014. Available at <blog.derbund.ch/zumrundenleder/blog/2014/01/09/es-leuchtete-und-schwebte-ueber-das-weserstadion/> [Accessed 7 March 2015]

50 'Misterio "cósmico" en San Lorenzo: ¿un OVNI sobrevoló el "Nuevo Gasómetro"?'. InfoBAE.com [online], 22 April 2014. Available at <www.infobae.com/2014/04/22/1559029-misterio-cosmico-san-lorenzo-un-ovni-sobrevolo-el-nuevo-gasometro> [Accessed 30 March 2015]

51 ' "UFO" spotted over London 2012 site'. BBC London [online], 10

November 2009. Available at <news.bbc.co.uk/local/london/hi/people_and_places/newsid_8352000/8352111.stm> [Accessed 10 March 2015]

52 Scott C. Waring (n.d.), 'US Presidents' [online]. Available at <www.ufosightingsdaily.com/p/us-presidents.html> [Accessed 10 March 2015] See also: Emily Smith (2009), 'UFO sees Obama become President', *The Sun* [online], n.d. Available at <www.thesun.co.uk/sol/homepage/news/article2165801.ece>. [Accessed 10 March 2015]

53 Benjamin Creme's Master (2013), comment to a report on Simona Bocchi's sighting. *Share International* magazine, Vol.32, No.3, p.12

54 Adamski (1955), op cit, p.68

55 Adamski (1957-58), op cit, Part 5, Question #96

56 Denaerde (1977), op cit, p.35

57 Adamski (1957-58), op cit, Part 4, Question #66

58 Giorgio Dibitonto (1990), *Angels in Starships*, p.8

59 Ibid., p.85

60 Denaerde (1977), op cit, p.88

61 Claudia Urbaczka (2012), 'UFO over German protest'. Letter to the editor, *Share International* magazine Vol.31, No.1, January/February 2012, p.33

62 Drishya Nair (2013), 'Mass UFO Sighting: Thousands watch "UFO" Hovering in Brazilian Skies during Protests'. *International Business Times* [online], 20 June. Available at <www.ibtimes.co.uk/mass-ufo-sighting-brazil-protests-aliens-truck-481193>; and Alejandro Rojas (2013), 'Protesters in Brazil film UFO while drone films protesters', Open Minds [online], 20 June. Available at <www.openminds.tv/protesters-film-ufo-while-drone-films-protesters-video-1057/22390>. [Accessed 14 March 2015] This sighting was confirmed as a spaceship from Venus by Benjamin Creme's Master in *Share International* magazine, Vol.32, No.7, September 2013, p.14

63 Arjun Walia (2013), 'Amazing Footage: Thousands Witness UFO over Brazilian Protests'. CE [online], 20 June. Available at <www.collective-evolution.com/2013/06/20/thousands-witness-amazing-ufo-over-brazilian-protests/> [Accessed 14 March 2015]

64 Minnie Nair (2014), 'Mass UFO Sighting: Spaceship Shoots up Vertically during Hong Kong protests'. *International Business Times* [online], 3 October. Available at <www.ibtimes.co.in/mass-ufo-sighting-spaceship-shoots-vertically-during-hong-kong-protests-610489> [Accessed 14 March 2015]

65 Carlos Fredo (2012), 'OVNI sobre el volcán Popocatépetl, octubre 2012'. StarMedia [online], 2 November. Available at <noticias.starmedia.com/insolito/ovni-sobre-volcan-popocatepetl-octubre-2012.html> [Accessed 20 March 2015]

66 Siberian Times Reporter (2013), 'So did a UFO shoot down the famous Chelyabinsk meteorite last month?'. *The Siberian Times* [online], 28 February. Available at <siberiantimes.com/weird-and-wonderful/news-and-features/news/so-did-a-ufo-shoot-down-the-famous-chelyabinsk-meteorite-last-month/> [Accessed 20 March 2015]

67 Norman Byrd (2014), 'UFO caught "monitoring" International Space Station on live camera'. Examiner.com [online], 9 October. Available at <www.examiner.com/article/ufo-caught-monitoring-international-space-station-on-live-camera-video>. [Accessed 20 March 2015]

68 Michael Rundle (2015), 'UFOs Outside the International Space Station: Why Do We Keep Seeing Them?'. Huffington Post UK [online], 26 January. Available at <www.huffingtonpost.co.uk/2015/01/26/ufos-international-space-_n_6546998.html>. [Accessed 20 March 2015]

69 Mary-Ann Russon (2014), 'Nasa's Curiosity Rover Captures "Cigar-Shaped" UFO Orbiting Mars'. *International Business Times* [online], 13 May. Available at <www.ibtimes.co.uk/nasas-curiosity-rover-captures-cigar-shaped-ufo-orbiting-mars-1448451>. [Accessed 20 March 2015]

70 Scott C Waring (2014), 'Dark UFO On Mars Caught by Curiosity Rover, July 2014'. UFO Sightings Daily [online], 18 July. Available at <www.ufosightingsdaily.com/2014/07/dark-ufo-on-mars-caught-by-curiosity.html>. [Accessed 20 March 2015]

71 Jimmy Nsubuga (2014), 'Does this mystery white light captured by Nasa's Curiosity rover suggest there's life on Mars?'. *Metro UK* [online], 8 April. Available at <metro.co.uk/2014/04/08/does-this-mystery-white-light-captured-by-nasas-curiosity-rover-suggest-theres-life-on-mars-4692107/>. [Accessed 20 March 2015]

72 'Bright lights on dwarf planet Ceres perplex NASA scientists'. *The Sydney Morning Herald* [online], 27 February 2015. Available at <www.smh.com.au/technology/sci-tech/bright-lights-on-dwarf-planet-ceres-perplex-nasa-scientists-20150227-13qx5r.html>. [Accessed 20 March 2015]

73 'Huge UFO spotted on SOHO image'. UFO Sightings Hotspot blog [online], 1 March, 2015. Available at <ufosightingshotspot.blogspot.nl/2015/03/huge-ufo-spotted-on-soho-image-mar-01.html>. [Accessed 20 March 2015]

'Out of the mouth of babes...'

74 Creme (2010), op cit, p.16

75 Ibid., pp.22-23

76 Stephen Coan (2008), 'The day the aliens landed'. *The Witness* [online], 16 April. Available at <www.witness.co.za/index.php?showcontent &global[_id]=6379>. [Accessed 26 March 2015]

77 Cynthia Hind (1995), 'The Children of Ariel School'. *UFO AfriNews*, No.11, Feb. 1995, pp.19-22
78 Stéphane Allix (dir.; 2011), *Experiencers*. 13E Rue, France. Available at <www.youtube.com/watch?v=BHy58wMgsrU> [Accessed 26 March 2015]
79 *Tineke's paranormale wereld*, RTL4, the Netherlands (27 March 1996). Available at <www.youtube.com/watch?v=g41mxGQPp0k> [Accessed 26 March 2015]
80 Hind (1982), *UFOs – African Encounters*, pp.138-145
81 Rosie Jones (dir.; 2010), *Westall '66: A Suburban UFO Mystery*. Screen Australia, Film Victoria, Endangered Pictures, Australia.
82 Roger Marsh (2015), '1966: Michigan children discover landed UFO in local field'. MUFON Case No. 63749, 13 March. Available at <www.mufon.com/ufo-news/-1966-michigan-children-discover-landed-ufo-in-local-field>. [Accessed 28 March 2015]
83 'Two children encounter UFO and small humanoid beings in Cussac, France'. UFO Evidence, n.d. Available at <www.ufoevidence.org/cases/case705.htm> [Accessed 28 March 2015]
84 Personal interview with Mr Falco Friedhoff, Amsterdam, the Netherlands, 4 April 2014

George Adamski (p.5)

a Timothy Good (2000), *Unearthly Disclosure*, p.256
b Ibidem, p.262
c Robert Chapman (1972), *UFO – Flying Saucers over Britain?*, 1974 reprint, p.115
d Waveney Girvan (1960), 'The Adamski Photographs – an open challenge'. *Flying Saucer Review*, Vol.6, No.2, March-April, p.4, quoting from a letter from Joseph N. Mansour of November 1954
e Waveney Girvan (1955), Letter to the Editor. *The Observer* newspaper, October 25; Desmond Leslie (1955), Foreword to Adamski's *Inside the Space Ships*, p.23.
f Interview with William Sherwood in M. Hesemann (1996), *UFOs: The Contacts – The Pioneers of Space*.
g Good (1998), *Alien Base*, p.155

2. Earth's cosmic isolation: A self-imposed confinement

One summer evening in the mid-1960s Dutch businessman Ad (short for Adrian) Beers and his family were sailing the Oosterscheldt, a large estuary in the south west of Holland, when his yacht's compass seemed broken. While sailing back to the harbour, he was suddenly staring into a strong blue-white searchlight. Switching the engine into reverse, full power, could not prevent the boat hitting something solid. Upon closer inspection it seemed as if Mr Beers' boat had hit the hull of an overturned ship and he saw a body floating in the water nearby. As he jumped overboard with a lifeline, he landed on a hard surface at a depth of just about one metre. Shortly after he had secured the lifeline to the floating body someone in a similar outfit as the drowning person, which looked like a space suit, came wading through the water to assist him in his rescue efforts. He then describes how the sight of an "animal-like face, with large square pupils in the eyes, which were both hypnotic and self-assured" struck him like a thunderbolt.

It was only then that he realised they were visitors from another planet who, out of gratitude for his rescue efforts, offered to share with him detailed information about their world. Over the course of two days he was invited to come down into the semi-submerged craft where he was shown vivid images of the way society on 'Iarga', as they called their planet, was organised, accompanied by detailed explanations of the underlying philosophy. Understandably, it was a life-changing experience for Mr Beers that would shake his worldview to the core.

Being the director-general of the Dutch importer for Swedish lorry manufacturer Scania, Mr Beers presented his story as science fiction under the pseudonym of Stefan Denaerde (a contraction of 'Stef van de Aarde' or 'Steve of Earth') in a 1969 book which became a bestseller that saw many reprints. In 1977 the first English edition was published as *Operation Survival Earth*, while a revised and expanded English edition was published in 1982 by the late Wendelle Stevens as *Contact from Planet Iarga*.

Thoroughly impressed by what he had been shown and told, when their exchange came to a close Mr Beers/Stefan Denaerde asked his contacts from space if they could provide more specific technological knowledge to advance Earth's civilization. The reply could not have been more straightforward: "The last thing that you need is technological information to increase the gap between your intellectual development and your almost non-existent social development. Carry on playing with your Mars probes for the moment, as half of your world's population lives in poverty and hunger. The only information you need lies in the field of societal standards."[1]

This, according to his contacts, is also the reason why humanity has been in cosmic isolation for millennia: "You do not have the values, the ethics, of a developed civilization. (…) It blocks the way to cosmic integration."[2]

Despite several claims to the contrary – that an elite group is in possession of space travel technology and have basically established a 'breakaway' civilization with the aim of controlling humanity and the world's resources – many others have been told the same thing as Denaerde. Let us remind ourselves here that, based on his contacts with one of the Masters of Wisdom, Benjamin Creme has said that although a number of governments have achieved some degree of 'anti-gravity' technology, none have actually "achieved the complete control of space (…) as is demonstrated by our Space Brothers".[3] And as recently as 2008, Apollo 14 astronaut Dr Edgar Mitchell, who says of himself that he is "privileged enough to be in on the fact that we have been visited on this planet", said in an interview: "I suspect that in the last 60 years or so there has been some back-engineering (…) but it is not nearly as sophisticated yet as what the apparent visitors have."[4]

Based on these corroborating statements, and the inconvenient fact that the elite already own the majority of wealth on this planet, which gives them undue influence on the democratic and judicial processes of many nations, as we shall see below, I think it is safe to file the 'secret space programme' claims, in the sense of members of Earth humanity travelling around the solar system in home grown craft, under 'Speculation' at best.

Enrique Barrios, who was asked to write his book *Ami, Child of the Stars* as a story for children, was told that a selfish race has no true intelligence: "They never reach the scientific level necessary to leave their planets and go on to invade other worlds. It's easier to build bombs than to build intergalactic ships … and if a civilization has no kindness and manages to attain a high scientific level, sooner or later it will use its destructive power against itself, long before it can leave for other worlds."[5] And about Earth in particular, "The mathematical relationship between science and love is terribly weighted toward the side of science; millions of civilizations like this one have self-destructed. This is a moment of change, a very dangerous one."[6]

Barrios' contact said that everything is interrelated, but

Top left: Mr Beers' *tjalk*, a typical Dutch flat-bottom barge with characteristic spritsail, which he sailed into a submerged UFO.
Bottom left: Mr Beers/Stefan Denaerde interviewed for Dutch KRO TV on the beach of the Oosterscheldt estuary in 1969.

Below: Dutch contactee Ad Beers/Stefan Denaerde (left) with UFO researcher Wendelle Stevens. (Photo: Brit Elders)

"that we [humanity] don't understand the law that ties everything together ... or that we don't *want* to see it"[7], while George Adamski was told: "Living in peace with one's fellowman is but a matter of understanding and compassion. It is a Universal Law we all must learn and apply in our daily contacts with others if we are to progress."[8] Amicizia-contactee Bruno Sammaciccia, too, was told: "This is a critical point in your history; a turning point in your technologies, but because of your childish enthusiasms you are forgetting your moral values. That would be a pity if you forget them, because everything arises from morality, and everything is done because of it."[9] He himself wrote: "They [the space visitors] put their moral [before] their technique, while here we do just the opposite."[10]

These statements are no less true as when Maitreya, who is #43 expected by many as the World Teacher for the New Age, pointed out Earth's enduring tragedy with rather more urgency in 1978: "Throughout the world there are men, women and little children who have not even the essentials to stay alive; they crowd the cities of many of the poorest countries in the world. This crime fills Me with shame. My brothers, how can you watch these people die before your eyes and call yourselves men?"[11]

That this natural law, this balance, which is so skewed toward the material – be it in science, politics, or economics – at the expense of our relating as brothers and sisters of the one humanity, is nothing new was pointed out by George Adamski numerous times: "All great teachers have taught the law of respect, love, and brotherhood. Jesus, whose teachings are the basis of every denomination of the Christian world, gave us one commandment... the commandment of love without judgment. Yet look at the divisions, resentments and hatreds prevalent amongst the people on Earth; all of which have laid the foundation for wars and rumors of wars confronting us on every

The World Teacher? No, not another religion!

The idea of the evolution of consciousness as a function of Life and a fact of Nature was first brought to public attention in modern times by H.P. Blavatsky in her works *Isis Unveiled* (1877) and *The Secret Doctrine* (1888). She re-acquainted mankind with the notion of the spiritual kingdom that has evolved out of the human kingdom, which consists of the Masters and Initiates of Wisdom, also known as the great White Lodge or, in Christian terms, the Kingdom of God.

According to these teachings of the Ageless Wisdom, of which Blavatsky's work represents the preparatory phase, at the beginning of every cosmic age this spiritual hierarchy sends a Teacher from their midst into the world, to inspire humanity of that time with a new revelation about the spiritual reality behind our physical existence. Their teachings have invariably been formed into religions by their followers because of humanity's lack of individuality and intellectual development.

George Adamski was well aware of this Law of Cyclic Appearance of teachers, when he spoke about "the Universal Laws which have been handed down throughout the centuries by the Men of Wisdom"[a]. In fact, he was one of several students of the Masters of Wisdom who studied with them in Tibet. The insights gained in his study formed the basis for his first book, *Wisdom of the Masters of the Far East,* which he published in 1936. Other teachers who studied with the Masters, in addition to H.P. Blavatsky, include Rolf Alexander M.D., Murdo MacDonald-Bayne and Baird T. Spalding.[b]

This recurring revelation by a new Teacher is known as the Doctrine of the Coming One and is evinced in almost every religion as the expected return of a teacher: Christians are waiting for the Second Coming, Jews are still expecting the Messiah, Buddhists await the fifth Buddha, Hindus the tenth incarnation of Vishnu, or Kalki Avatar, and segments of Islam are awaiting the twelfth Mahdi, or Imam Mahdi.

While several of the early contactees talked about the Second Coming in mystical terms of a subjective experience on a mass scale, the Italian contactee Giorgio Dibitonto was told in 1980: "No single event that ever yet happened on Earth can compare with that which stands before you now. (...) You will be led by a new Moses whom we all love and admire greatly. He will lead all the people on this new exodus, like a good brother or father."[c] Indeed, the Tibetan Master Djwhal Khul announced in 1948 that, as a result of humanity's suffering during the World Wars of the 20th century, the Christ had decided "to re-appear or return to visible Presence on Earth as soon as possible".[d]

According to the teachings, a World Teacher, under whichever name his followers recognize him, usually manifests by overshadowing the consciousness of a disciple, in the way that the Buddha worked through Prince Gautama and the Christ worked through Jesus in Palestine. It seems George Adamski knew about this distinction, when he wrote in 1962: "...Jesus was a personality and Christ is conscious consciousness or cosmic consciousness. Jesus, as an individual, schooled himself to permit [Christ's] consciousness to express through his form..."[e] Students of the Ageless Wisdom teaching are well aware that until 1929 the later educator and philosopher Jiddu Krishnamurti was being prepared as a possible vehicle for the manifestation of the World Teacher for the New Age.

As a contactee, British author and esotericist Benjamin Creme gave talks about the spiritual mission of the Space Brothers in the 1950s and from 1974 began his mission to inform the world that this time the World Teacher would come himself.

According to Creme, Maitreya, which he says is the personal name of the World Teacher, arrived in London as his centre in the modern world in July 1977 and has since been preparing mankind and the world for his open manifestation at the earliest possible moment.

Creme has always maintained that the Teacher has not come as a religious leader, or to create followers to be 'saved', but to teach humanity the Art of Self-realisation (see also page 129) and to establish right human relations as the basis for a new dispensation. Creme's latest information [July 2015] is that the long-awaited Day of Declaration could take place within one-and-a-half year, but most likely when the current economic and financial systems have collapsed.[f]

Notes on page 81

44

side. If the people on other planets had lived their teachings no better than Earthlings, they, too, would be experiencing the same turmoil we find around us today."[12] According to Enrique Barrios' character Ami, however, there is greater unhappiness now on Earth than in previous times, because "[p]eople were less sensitive then, they suffered less from the atrocities, they believed in war. Today they no longer do so."[13]

Stefan Denaerde's contacts, too, referred to the teachings of Jesus when they said: "You don't have to construct complicated comparisons in order to discover who is rich and who is not. One-half of the world is busy with slimming cures and the other half is suffering from malnutrition and hunger. The words of Christ regarding this leave no room for doubt: 'For I was hungry and you gave me to eat; I was thirsty and you gave me to drink. Verily I say unto you, inasmuch as you did it for one of the least of these, you did it for me.'"[14]

In a vivid illustration of the situation we find ourselves in today, Barrios writes: "When the scientific level overwhelms the level of love in a world, that world self-destructs. There is a mathematical relationship... If a world's level of love is low, there is collective unhappiness, hatred, violence, division, wars, and a dangerously high level of destructive capacity."[15] Hence, one of Adamski's Martian contacts exhorts us: "Now that your scientific knowledge has so far outstripped your social and human progress, the gap between *must* be filled with urgent haste."[16]

Likewise, Daniel Fry, author of *The White Sands Incident*, was told: "Your own philosophers, both past and present, have given to your people ample instructions. Ample wisdom to enable them to chart the proper course, if they will only realize the absolute necessity of following it. (...) There are many statements in your books of religion and philosophy which show that the great thinkers of your race, down through the ages, have been well aware of the dangers of concentration on material science."[17] So, "unless some ways and means are found to stimulate the growth of the spiritual and social sciences on your earth, a time will inevitably come when your emphasis on those matters which are material will cause your civilization to collapse. Ruin and destruction will then be brought to both the spiritual and social side of your civilization."[18]

Echoing Denaerde's contacts' refusal to share more techno-logical knowledge, 1950s US contactee Orfeo Angelucci was told: "To add to the destructive phase of man's scientific knowledge is not permitted. We are working now to turn that knowledge to constructive purposes upon Earth. Also we hope to give men a deeper knowledge and understanding of their own true nature and a greater awareness of the evolutionary crisis facing them."[19]

This evolutionary crisis is a crisis of human consciousness: while inwardly we know we are one species, one race, outwardly, because the relatively new-found quality of individuality in mankind has such a strong appeal, a sense of separation has provoked the fiercest competition among individual members of the human race to the point where the world's richest *80 individuals* are wealthier than the poorest *50 per cent of humanity* and, according to Oxfam, by 2016 the richest one percent of humanity will own more than the remaining 99 per cent combined, with more than a billion people still living on less than $1.25 a day.[20]

The World Teacher, through his associates, called this gross inequality a 'tumor': "Not only large financial institutions which are tumbling into bankruptcy; the whole world is becoming bankrupt – mentally and spiritually. The world is going through a huge crisis and all the medicines have been tried and failed. The tumour has to burst open before the healing can begin."[21]

"Switch on the news and you see record-breaking protests, historic uprisings and riots on once-calm streets – there's no doubt that growing income inequality is an issue of central importance."[22]

This is not a quote from a recent article about the need for social change, but the opening statement of chapter 2 in the *Outlook on the Global Agenda 2014* report from the World Economic Forum, best known for its annual meeting of the global elite in Davos, Switzerland. World leaders are finally becoming more aware of the dangers of the enormous, and widening, gap between rich and poor, and that this trend cannot be allowed to continue unchecked was also reflected in President Obama's State of the Union speech of January 2014: "Today, after four years of economic growth, corporate profits and stock prices have rarely been higher, and those at the top have never done better. But average wages have barely budged. Inequality has deepened. (…) The cold, hard fact is that even in the midst of recovery, too many Americans are working more than ever just to get by – let alone get ahead." He then went on to outline policies meant to address the dangers inherent in the growing disparity in income and opportunity.[23] While a growing movement for living wages has since gained momentum and achieved some successes, the difference in income between the rich and the rest remains obscene by any standard.

One way in which people with a heart and some common sense often express their disbelief about humanity's dysfunctional ways of relating to itself and the planet is by taking the perspective of an outsider: "If a Martian were to visit our planet…" followed by an observation of the way humans have complicated life for themselves or other creatures that makes no sense on any level beyond a profit motive.

While many readers will be aware that we have been visited and are being visited by people from other planets, many may not know exactly how often these same visitors have voiced their concerns about the way we have chosen to organise society around the need to earn money for daily living and pursuing the "dream" of limitless wealth, no matter if it kills the planet. For instance, in 1954, during his sojourn on a mothership, George Adamski was told by his hosts from space: "If man is to live without catastrophe, he must look upon his fellow being as himself, the one a reflection of the other."[24] After many years of sustained contact with the people from other planets Adamski added in December 1964: "[T]o have a healthy and prosperous society, that which causes the most trouble must be removed. As we all know, this stigma is poverty in the midst of plenty. It is the cause of sickness, crime, and the many evils that we know..."[25]

Writing about the state of the world some 60 years ago, Adamski's observations now have an almost prophetic quality to them: "Today many people are living in hell right here, because of the confusions, uncertainties and divisions; all of which create fear, want and hatred."[26] For if anyone questioned the validity of that observation in 1957, when he wrote these words, they are now a painful reality in the newspapers' descriptions of the effects of government policies to 'balance the budget', 'stimulate the economy' or 'reassure the markets'.

This didn't happen overnight, but is the culmination of a trend that people in developed nations of the world have long known about and that has found its way into political discourse and economic policy since the neoliberal agenda became prevalent, as I have pointed out elsewhere, with the election of Margaret Thatcher in the UK in 1979 and Ronald Reagan in the USA in 1980, whose administrations laid the groundwork for the notion that a smaller government, and less market regulation, is a better government. Over the past four decades this concept of government has been embraced even by social democratic and many left-wing parties in European countries, although the US version is still the most radical, with only minor differences in Democratic and Republican views on the government's 'responsibility' to spend as little on public services as possible.

Towards the end of World War II, during his State of the Union speech on 11 January 1944 President Franklin D. Roosevelt outlined what has become known as the 'second Bill of Rights', which included "The right to a useful and remunerative job in the industries or shops or farms or mines of the Nation; the right to earn enough to provide adequate food and clothing and recreation; (…) the right of every family to a decent home; the right to adequate medical care and the opportunity to achieve and enjoy good health; the right to adequate protection from the economic fears of old age, sickness, accident, and unemployment; the right to a good education".[27] Many of these were later incorporated in the Universal Declaration of Human Rights, championed by FDR's widow Eleanor Roosevelt and ratified by the United Nations Organisation on 10 December 1948.[28]

FDR's commitment to human freedom from want and true liberty to pursue happiness was reinforced by President Lyndon B. Johnson's 'Great Society', launched in 1964, which was primarily focused on the elimination of poverty and racial injustice in the USA. By 1970, six years on from its launch, "the portion of Americans living below the poverty line dropped from 22.2 percent to 12.6 percent, the most dramatic decline over such a brief period in this century,"[29] according to former Secretary of Health, Education and Welfare Joseph Califano Jr. In his 1999 article 'What Was Really Great About The Great Society – The truth behind the conservative myths' he enumerates the many achievements of a set of government interventions that "saw government as providing a hand up, not a handout", through education, health care and affirmative action as tools for creating social justice.

As if confirming this view, in the second, expanded English edition of his book, Stefan Denaerde says: "Their definition of the word civilization or culture has nothing to do with the scientific or technological development level, but with the manner in which the community takes care of the handicapped or weaker beings. The word superculture defines the situation that arises when through individual effort, a group structure has arisen which abolishes any discrimination against any individual."[30]

While most of the Western world was in the process of post-war reconstruction, the space visitors already foresaw what might be one of the flaws inherent in our socio-economic system, even before the neoliberal return to 19th century capitalism. In 1955 a Saturnian Master described humanity's state of moral starvation to George Adamski rather poetically: "...man, in his lack of understanding, has destroyed the harmony of his being on your Earth. He dwells in enmity with his neighbor, his mind divided in confusion. Peace he has never known; true beauty he has not seen. No matter how he prides himself on his material achievements, he lives still as a lost soul. And who is this man that dwells in such darkness? He is the mortal one who has failed to serve the Immortal One! ... It is he who fears all things beyond the understanding of his fettered mind. It is he who has denied the hunger of his spirit."[31]

But instead of giving expression to our essential oneness, for instance through the implementation of the proposals of the commission founded and led by former German Chancellor Willy Brandt, to address the disparity in the distribution of global wealth and opportunity, Western nations as the dominant exponents of humanity at the time began the process of giving market forces free reign, by liberalizing markets – that is, removing regulations and restrictions for the protection of citizens and consumers – and selling off public services that had been built from their nation's wealth and taxpayers' contributions, such as electricity networks, public transportation, postal services, health care, housing and even the water supply, to large corporations that now operate or trade them for profit.

In his article 'Sale of the century: the privatisation scam', British writer and journalist James Meek describes how we got to that point: "The market belief system, which holds that government is incompetent by default, that state taxation is oppressive, that the desire for wealth is the right and principal motivator of achievement and that virtually all human wants can best be met by competing private firms, was becoming entrenched in the non-communist world, from Chile to New Zealand. Made bold by a popular public perception that government overspending and selfish organised labour were to blame for economic stagnation and high inflation in the 1970s, Thatcher and Reagan had taken on powerful trade unions, and won. Barriers to the international movement of goods and money had fallen; the European Union was, on paper, a single marketplace. In Britain, restrictions on how much ordinary people could borrow to finance their everyday needs had been scrapped, and millions had acquired credit cards. Volumes of regulations controlling how banks were allowed to use people's deposits had been torn up, and unimaginably vast sums were being moved privately from country to country. Government spending had been cut, as had income tax and corporation tax. Sales tax and fees for everyday services had been raised. Council houses [social housing; GA] and big state enterprises had been privatised, with more on the way, leading to hundreds of thousands of redundancies. Thatcher's programme in Britain was an inspiration for the IMF and the World Bank as they experimented with the conditions they attached to bail-out loans to developing countries."[32]

Well before the coming to power of this neoliberal world view, Mr Denaerde's contacts told him in 1965 of the dangers of unregulated market forces, that the 'free' economy existed "based on the law of the jungle, the right of the economically strong or the status quo of the balance of power, which made military power a necessity. A highly technical culture is controlled by a number of natural laws, one of which states: discrimination can only exist temporarily, supported by other discriminations. Every discrimination leads to others. Power is discrimination by the strong against the weak and is part of the law of the jungle."[33]

The consequences of this shift from working towards a society that is free and just for all to an economy where everyone is competing for a hypothetical chance to become a billionaire, while monetizing everything from education to the prison system, are devastating. Not only for the corruption of our democratic and judicial processes and institutions, or the debilitating effects of an unrelenting bombardment of commercials vying for our attention, which combine to disenfranchise and dumb down citizens and enables the global elite to 'rig the game' in their favour even further, but especially for those billions of people who are still left without the fundamental human requirements of food, housing, healthcare and education, as well as for a fast growing number of people who need two or more jobs to be able to afford the bare minimum of these basic needs.

In April 1989, with détente between the USA and the USSR in full swing, and shortly before the dramatic collapse of the Iron Curtain that separated the superpowers' sphere of influence in Europe, *Share International* magazine published a commentary from Maitreya, the World Teacher, through one of his close associates, that "in the last two to three years we have seen a reduction in wars and conflicts taking place throughout the world as the superpowers withdrew from their policy of supplying arms to further their own foreign aims and interests. The energy which drives soldiers into battle and fills the air with warplanes has been switched off." However, the World Teacher says, the energy found a new womb in commercialization, created by market forces: "The new creed of the superpowers has become the economy, which is the soul of commercialization, and this represents a serious new threat to the world, one that could even compromise human life. The quality of commercialization is greed, and it will affect all nations. This negative energy which recoiled from the battlefield is a force without eyes or mind and will create a very hostile world. But although the politicians believe that commercialization is the future of the human race they cannot control this energy. (...) We are now seeing a new battle taking place which can only be won if the human mind can divert this negative energy. Only awareness will stop this force and people will fight for survival if commercialization compromises human welfare and health. The situation will erupt like a volcano."[34]

Since those words were spoken several 'eruptions' have occurred, notably around the 'dot-com' bubble in 2000, and even more seriously in 2008, when the global financial system was facing a total meltdown as a result of rampant speculation by bankers whose prime motive was to earn their companies more money faster, so they would receive larger bonuses. The collapse of the Lehman Brothers bank in the USA affected the global banking system and major banks in most Western countries had to be bailed out of their debts to prevent a chain reaction that would have reduced the current financial system

Above: Flying saucer captured at Charles de Gaulle airport near Paris during take-off on board flight AF980/MK045 from Paris to Mauritius in October 2010.

Below: Flying saucer photographed by Dutch psychic Robbert van den Broeke, over a crop circle in a wheat field in Standdaarbuiten, Netherlands on 27 July 2009. (Photo: © Robbert van den Broeke)

to what experts know it actually is – a house of cards, but no longer standing. The banking crisis quickly caused a euro crisis in the European Union, which in turn turned into a debt crisis and a national budget crisis for many of its member states when the USA and the EU decided to use virtually unlimited credit to bail out private corporations (banks) that had been allowed to take virtually unlimited risks because governments had done away with regulations. While the bailouts have managed to create the appearance that the financial sector has been rescued from the brink, and it's almost business as usual – although a growing number of economic observers and analysts are warning for an even greater implosion in 2015 because none of the causes of the crises have been addressed – people around the world are still suffering the consequences of having been made to pay for these systemic injustices.

Readers may be interested to know in this respect that the space people whom Buck Nelson encountered in 1952 had little regard for speculators: "Some of our commonly used methods of making a living would be absolutely unacceptable to them. One of these methods is our practice of making money from money in so many different ways."[35] Truman Betherum was told very much the same thing by his contacts in 1955: "If we had them on Clarion it would soon be of small worth; we'd have mansions and slums, as you do."[36]

We have not only slums, but many homeless people, too. In the USA alone, the official Department of Housing and Urban Development's homelessness number in January 2014 was over 570,000, but the Department of Education puts the number of homeless children alone at 1.3 million in 2013.[37]

To illustrate what exactly the space people mean when they say we do not have the ethics of a developed civilization, it seems that homelessness itself is not disgraceful enough, as a newspaper report from October 2014 shows how, in the USA, "[m]any cities have chosen to criminally punish people living on the street for doing what any human being must do to survive..." One of the examples in the report is about a homeless man named Gil and the mind-boggling traffic violation for which he received a ticket in Fort Lauderdale, Florida: "In his hands is a police citation written a few weeks ago when an officer found him sitting on the kerb with his feet touching the road. 'Feet in Roadway Disturbing Traffic,' it reads." And on 22 October 2014 National Public Radio reports that since January 2013, 21 US cities passed measures "aimed at restricting the people who feed the homeless", either by introducing rules on the use of public property or requiring that those preparing and serving food to the homeless get a food handler's permit.[38] Three days after such an ordinance was passed by the city of Fort Lauderdale, Florida, 90-year-old Arnold Abbott, who had been feeding the homeless at a public beach for the past 23 years, was arrested.[39] A reader of the online report poignantly commented: "Jesus would be locked up in a jail cell if he came to America", reminding us of George Adamski's remark in 1958, when he asked: "What chance would Jesus have if He were to return to Earth in fulfilment of Bible Prophecy?"[40]

It is infuriating to read about injustice being passed on those who try to redress injustice, but we need to be aware, we need to 'want' to see it, as Enrique Barrios said, if we are to stand up for justice. There are countless other examples. One of the European countries hit especially hard by European austerity demands is Spain. Youth unemployment in the country stood at over 50 per cent in early 2015[41], while in 2014 the Roman Catholic charity Caritas alone distributed food, clothes and help to 2.5 million people, or 1 in 20 Spaniards.[42] Similar, or sometimes worse, statistics may be cited for Italy, Portugal,

Ireland, and Greece because the privatisation wave that was set in motion in the 1980s was forced on these countries by the EU and the World Bank as a condition for emergency loans which they needed as a result of the euro crisis that evolved from the banking crisis. Even as this chapter is being written [July 2015], the brave struggle of the Greek people against the imposition of austerity measures that would further tighten the financial grip of its European creditors and the International Monetary Fund (IMF) seems lost with the last minute agreement by the Greek government to secure a much needed bailout.

But increasingly, commentators are denouncing privatisation and the greater freedom for everyone it was supposed to bring as a scam. To give readers a quick impression of the huge imbalance that has been created in favour of corporate wealth at the cost of social justice, here are some key facts from an article by Owen Jones based on his book *The Establishment – And how they got away with it*: "More than £1tn of public money was poured into the banks following the financial collapse. The emergency package came with few government-imposed conditions and with little calling to account. (…) In 2012, 2,714 British bankers were paid more than €1m – 12 times as many as any other EU country." At the same time, "In the austerity programme that followed the financial crisis, state support for those at the bottom of society has been eroded. The support that remains is given with stringent conditions attached. 'Benefit sanctions' are temporary suspensions of benefits, often for the most spurious or arbitrary reasons. According to the government's figures, 860,000 benefit claimants were sanctioned between June 2012 and June 2013… According to the Trussell Trust, the biggest single provider of food banks, more than half of recipients were dependent on handouts owing to cuts or sanctions to their benefits."[43]

A harrowing example is found in a newspaper report which describes how a 59-year-old man in the UK suffering from diabetes, who had worked for 24 years, had lost his benefits and was found dead with a pile of CVs he had printed out for job applications lying close to his body. The Department for Work and Pensions' Jobcentre claimed he had not been serious enough looking for work and, following the tightening of the social benefits system in October 2012, had sanctioned him. According to the newspaper report, his younger sister, who had discovered the body, found that "his electricity had been cut off, meaning that the fridge where he kept his insulin was no longer working. There was very little left to eat in the flat – six tea bags, an out-of-date tin of sardines and a can of tomato soup. His pay-as-you-go mobile phone had just 5p [±10¢] credit left on it and he had only £3.44 [±$5.28] in his bank account. The autopsy notes reveal that his stomach was empty."[44] That this was not an isolated incident was underscored by the fact that the UK's statistics watchdog called on the Department for Work and Pensions to provide clear information after it had delayed the release of statistics on the number of benefit claimants who have died after they had their benefits cut or stopped.[45]

This is not even the full extent of the moral bankruptcy of our present systems, writes Owen Jones: "Much of Britain's public sector has now become a funding stream for profiteering companies. According to the National Audit Office (NAO), around half of the £187bn spent by the public sector on goods and services now goes on private contractors. (…) In 2012, £4bn of taxpayers' money was shovelled into the accounts of the biggest private contractors…" yet "tax avoidance is rampant among much of the corporate and wealthy elite that benefits so much from state handouts", running in the billions of pounds.

While these numbers pertain to the UK, the situation in

the USA is not fundamentally different, and hardly better in other Western countries. Hence, Mr Jones concludes: "Social security for the poor is shredded, stripped away, made ever more conditional. But welfare for large corporations and wealthy individuals is doled out like never before. The question is not just whether such an establishment is unjust: the question is whether it is sustainable."[46]

Again, the foresight of the space visitors is astounding, given what Stefan Denaerde wrote about the insights he was given in the mid-1960s: "Personal property is an indication of a very primitive level of culture. We had enough intelligence to build rockets, but not enough to see that the laws of the survival of the fittest and might is right must be abolished. Perhaps I could explain to them how I thought we could survive with such a system. Because though ours was a highly interesting system, what they had found here in discrimination beat anything that they had ever encountered before. Earth people seem to be continually occupied with thinking of new discriminations, and using them as solutions to the ones that already exist."[47]

With the inequality built into the world economic system now affecting people in the developed part of the world as well as those in developing nations, protests are increasing around the globe. In many northern European countries, where the remains of the social equality policies of the 1960s and 1970s have absorbed much of the effects of austerity measures so far, the public's disaffection with the political class thus far expresses mainly as fear of 'the other' aimed at immigrants and refugees that are seen as threats to their countries' social security systems. And while such xenophobia is certainly not absent in southern European countries, several have seen the swift rise of new political movements. In Greece, a broad coalition was formed

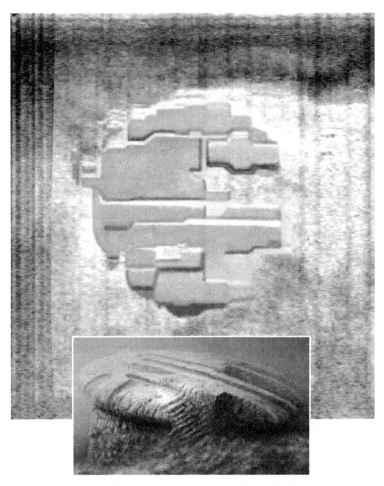

In 2011 Peter Lindberg and Dennis Asberg, members of the Swedish Ocean X diving company, discovered a circular or crescent-shaped object of 60m in diameter and 4m in height and a 1,500m trail in the Baltic Sea, at a depth of about 90m. A smaller disc-shaped object was discovered at about 400m distance from the larger object.

According to information coming from Benjamin Creme (*Share International* magazine July/August 2012), both objects are replicas of Martian craft that were deliberately released by the Space Brothers. (Inset: Artistic rendering by Hauke Vagt; thebalticanomaly.se) under the name Syriza, which was swept to power in the March 2015 elections, while in Spain the new Podemos political party originated from the 'Indignados' protests in 2009 and is poised for a major electoral victory in Spain's next parliamentary elections, even though the country has introduced draconian anti-demonstration laws to curb the anti-austerity protests.

So this 'freedom' that commercialization was supposed to bring is actually enslaving us. The mantra of governments since the 1980s has been that in order to increase the wealth of a country, the richest should be allowed to use as much of their wealth for their own benefit, since wealth creates wealth. Although not founded on any proven economic theory, this was implemented in government policies to slash taxes for the wealthiest members of society and subsidize major industries, even if they are obsolete already, such as the defence industry and fossil fuel and nuclear industries. There is now no society on Earth which does not experience the detrimental and dangerous consequences of such institutionalised discrimination between rich and poor, although the space visitors already warned against such social segregation to Mr Denaerde in 1965 when it was far less obvious to us: "The most dangerous natural law governing the development of an intelligent people states: a highly technological society does away with all discrimination or self-destructs. To supply technical information to a people like yourselves is a serious crime against the cosmic laws."[48]

The dangers referred to here lie in the fact that we have used competition as an integral building block of how we structure our lives. As Mr Denaerde is told: "The selfish behavior of the masses, where everyone takes everything they can, prevents the ability to work for the common good – to create, for example, a clean planet where the balance of nature can be maintained for an unlimited time. It is also impossible to limit the use of natural resources for the sake of future generations, because a selfish person cannot give up anything for someone else."[49]

The words of Enrique Barrios' protagonist Ami come to mind here, who says: "The problem is not in the people, but in the systems they use. People have evolved, but systems have remained backward. Bad systems make good people suffer. These systems make people unhappy, which finally turns them bad. A good system of global organization can easily turn bad into good."[50] As if confirming the statements made by Denaerde's space contacts, Ami says: "...with the right information and stimulus, and within an appropriate system of social organisation, people stop being thoughtless – they stop being 'bad'. Therefore, police are no longer needed." When his young friend Pedro replies: "Incredible!", Ami responds: "Not really. What *is* incredible is that in your world brothers kill brothers..."[51]

In our current world system, Ami observes, the best are rewarded, while "the rest are humiliated and the winners' egos grow..." but, he explains, to win actually means "to be more than the rest, again, competition, egoism, division. Competition should be against yourself, to outdo yourself, and not against the other brothers and sisters. Those things don't exist in maternal, evolved worlds, because therein lies the seed of war and destruction."[52] In an article on the true purpose of education, American educator Alfie Kohn made an incisive distinction when he said: "Our society's infatuation with the word competitiveness ... exacerbates the problem by encouraging a confusion between two very different ideas: excellence and the desperate quest to triumph over other people."[53] George Adamski had conveyed a very similar notion in 1965 when he was asked the question, "Without competition like we have on Earth would not all initiative be stifled?" His answer was: "No, if anything it would be stimulated. A free enterprise would still be a free enterprise... The spirit of competition could easily be replaced by an individual's desire to do the best he can according to his ability."[54]

When people talk of 'healthy competition', esotericist Benjamin Creme calls it a rationalization: " 'Healthy competition' simply brings down the price of a product... There is no advantage if a product is created cheaply by competition between hundreds of firms, all producing the same thing, if the process involves commercialization, thus diminishing the quality of life. (...) You cannot cost a product only on a dollar index; you have to look at the social result of producing it. Is it right to squander and misuse the resources needed to build 100 different types of automobiles, drain-pipes, doors, or whatever, in order to get to the lowest possible price, if the social, global and ecological costs are devastating? (...) 'Healthy competition' makes an excess of everything, and then the producers compete to sell the product. However, we cannot buy everything. This is where the myth of choice comes in."[55]

Stefan Denaerde relates his space contacts' assessment of what we do under the guise of 'advertising' and 'public relations' to convince consumers to choose one product or service over another, which in their eyes borders on indecency: "A continual stream of seemingly new models compelled our status-symbol oriented society to discard things before they had reached the end of their useful life. A terrible waste of raw material and production capacity, and, even worse, it was a stimulant for jealousy and greed, and this was criminal. This promotion of materialism, a deadly danger for an intelligent race, was directly opposed to any idea of justice." Not only that, but our advertising is regarded by the space visitors as "a despicable form of propaganda which was ethically unacceptable. In a socially stable society, you had not only freedom of speech, but, even more important, freedom of thought. Propaganda, repeated one-sided information, damaged the freedom of thought, and that was unacceptable discrimination."[56]

Canadian UFO researcher and contactee Wilbert B. Smith provides another poignant example of how long we have been struggling with the same problems. In his article 'The Battle of Man's Mind', he writes: "...no matter how hard we may all strive to be strong-minded and individualistic, we are all subtly influenced by the spoken and written word and other forms of thought communication, particularly through the medium of books, newspapers, radio and television. In the latter field, as the sponsors know only too well, even the 'commercials' play an important role in making up our minds to purchase certain products. In our business and social lives, we are often swayed by the thoughts of others and some people too apathetic to form opinions themselves, are willing to accept the views of others more articulate, as their own. (...) In the field of politics, often an area of great misrepresentation in order to gain votes, even greater pressures are brought to bear and we are often influenced by the seemingly convincing rhetoric of clever politicians. But it is in the area of international politics that the gravest dangers lie, for here the stakes are high and the lust for power the greatest."[57]

A good example in the context of this chapter is the Iraq War (2003-2011), which was started by the USA and the UK under the false accusation of Iraq's involvement with the terrorist attack on the World Trade Center in New York City in 2001 and it stocking weapons of mass destruction, and when there was an unprecedented public condemnation with 12.5 million people worldwide marching in protest of the looming invasion[58], it was re-sold as an act of kindness, with a 'coalition of the willing' bringing Iraq freedom and democracy from the barrel of cannons, while it was really about securing Iraq's oil reserves for

US industrial interests at rock bottom rates.

As this chapter shows, so prevalent have we allowed the concept of competition to become, that we now accept it – to our own detriment – as a fact of life even when it comes to our labour, with millions of people in countries all over the world who can only find jobs at below the minimum wage level. Because we revere competition, and low prices, we are left to compete for jobs at the lowest possible wages, so increasingly we can't even make a decent living unless we are prepared to work two or more jobs, leaving people no time for relaxation, let alone self-development or self-realization.

The separation between the (relatively) wealthy and destitute that divided the world in North and South for many decades, is now dividing every nation. Around the world migrants are clamouring to enter regions where they expect to be able to earn a living, for which they are prepared to take on jobs that the locals find beneath them, without any job security, with no safeguards for dangerous work and at less-than-minimum pay. Yet, no measure of bureaucratic rules, personal identification, international or national restrictions on immigration, or even walls or seas seem capable of stopping these brothers and sisters from claiming their right to a marginally more decent life.

Still many of us, especially elected representatives of the people, are convinced – by ideology or by the lure of greater wealth or power after leaving office – that more freedom for private corporations is the key to making life better for those at the bottom, thereby shackling freedom and increasing injustice for individuals who aren't wealthy enough to 'buy' these 'commodities' in the marketplace. So with efforts to force liberalizations upon indebted countries, with Greece and Puerto Rico as the most recent examples, that favour corporate interests over social security and that introduce even farther-reaching liberties for multinational corporations which undermine democratic processes even further in the form of the TTIP and TTP trade agreements, it should not surprise us that it will take another, complete meltdown of our current financial and economic systems for enough people to recognize the need to stand up against inequality, injustice and economic slavery on a global scale.

Benjamin Creme's Master put it most eloquently, when he said: "Commercialization, that burgeoning but stealthy and often hidden menace, controls now the lives and destiny of countless millions, and reduces to a cypher the God-given individuality of man. People are now statistics without purpose or needs, pawns on the chess-board of market forces and company profits."[59]

However, as the Master from Venus told George Adamski: "There is but *one* life. That life is all-inclusive, and until men of Earth realize that they cannot serve or live two lives, but only one, they will be constantly opposing one another. That is one major truth that *must* be learned by all Earth men before life on your world can match life on other planets."[60]

Having lost sight of the Oneness of all life, even of our oneness as brothers and sisters of the human race, we have convinced ourselves that we are separated from the Creator, lost the connection with our planet and the essence of our being, our souls; we have turned against each other and have turned life itself into a competition for survival. In the words of one of the six men on the Saturnian mothership whom Adamski met during his first visit to a mothership in February 1953: "So long as you live this way, divided one against the other, your sorrows will be multiplied. For when you seek your brother's life, someone seeks yours. This is the meaning of the words once spoken by Jesus of Nazareth. Remember that he said: 'Put up again thy sword into its place: for all they who take the sword shall perish with the sword.' The truth of these words has been proven throughout the history of man on Earth."[61]

So far the choices we have made have wreaked havoc even in the environment that we depend on for our existence. In his interview on BTV, the first commercial TV channel in Bulgaria, in 2012 Professor Lachezar Filipov, who is now heading an international research project into the crop circle phenomenon, says that people are being paid to make crop circle hoaxes to create confusion "so that this information would not be taken seriously". He states unreservedly that this is the reason the fossil fuel interests continue to damage the planet for, if we have proof that extraterrestrials exist, this means that there are other alternatives to our technological development: "Business prefers that we consume what we have on Earth so that those that earn the money continue to stockpile it. If for example we have access to the pure energy, the space energy, then we have to forget about gas, coal and others..."[62]

After all, Brazilian contactee Dino Kraspedon was told, the saucer technology could "lead to man's complete liberation and the release from the 'patriotic' chains that bind him, and the reinstatement of his right to direct his own life which a misguided social order deprived him of, leading him by various 'isms' to a criminal and unbrotherly clash of interests. The petroleum reserves of Earth are running out, fissionable material will one day come to an end and with deforestation, rivers and waterfalls will dry up, but atmospheric pressure will always be there."[63]

Being so confused about the nature and purpose of Life, it should come as no surprise that we have lost contact with the human races in the rest of the solar system, lost sight of their reality, and thereby imposed a cosmic isolation on ourselves. In February 1953 the Venusian Master told Adamski: "We would gladly give you this knowledge [of overcoming gravity] which has served us so well, except that you have not yet learned to live with one another in peace and brotherhood, for the welfare of all men alike, as we have on other worlds."[64]

However, as it stands, the Venusian Master continued, "If we revealed this power to you or to any Earth man and it became public knowledge, some of your people would quickly build ships for space traveling, mount guns upon them and go on a shooting spree in an attempt to conquer and take possession of other worlds." And, "Earth men will not be allowed to come in numbers or to remain, until they have learned to embrace the all-inclusive life as lived by people of other worlds, rather than the selfish personal life as found on Earth today."

We have come to value our individuality so highly that we spurn unity for fear of uniformity. In the current political climate in the United States even the suggestion of placing the common good before individual freedoms is seen by many as the threat of Nazism. Yet, the pursuit of unity is intrinsic to man, which starts with our need to belong – to our own family, a sports club, a church, a political party, a nation, et cetera. What demagogues, power-hungry individuals, or those who fear them forget, however, is that this natural pursuit can only be successful if it is based on respect for individual differences, since uniformity goes against the natural order. Hence, the aim should be for unity in diversity, where strength in numbers is matched and reinforced by the contribution of our individual talents to the whole.

As Adamski's Martian contact Firkon said: "We of other worlds who have been living unrecognized amongst you can see clearly how identity with Divine origin has been lost.

People of Earth have become separate entities which are no longer truly human in expression as in the beginning they were. Now they are but slaves of habit. Nonetheless, imprisoned within these habits is still the original soul that yearns for expression according to its Divine inheritance. This smothering urge is bound to disturb deeply the man chained to his ruts by the mechanism of habit. And this is why, desiring finer and greater expression, more often than men realize, something stirring within the depths of their beings leaves the habit-bound self uneasy and restless. (…) [U]ntil man can cast off the shackles of his personal self-pride (…) he will continue to live as a warrior against the laws of his own being."[65]

Not for nothing, writes Benjamin Creme's Master, "The arid desert which we call the modern world leaves men bereft of that which makes them human: happy, creatively fulfilled, quick to respond to each other's needs, and free. Deadly competition corrodes the human spirit and now sits in judgement on the 'battle' of life. Life, the Great Adventure, has been corrupted and replaced by an agonizing and unfair struggle for mere survival."[66]

The Venusian Master explained it thus: "Understanding of the universal laws both uplifts and restricts. As it is now with us, so it could be on your Earth. Lifted up by your knowledge, this same understanding would make it impossible to move in violence against your brothers. You would know that the same conviction, inherent in every individual being, which makes him feel that he has the divine privilege of directing his own life and shaping his own destiny, even though it be by the path of trial and error, applies equally to any group, nation, or race of mankind."[67] True progress, the Master adds, "is happiness and lies all along the upward pathway from its beginning. And happiness makes men brothers in tolerance toward another man's efforts, even though of a different nature from their own."[68]

Being self-imposed, our cosmic isolation need not be permanent, but its termination depends on our ability to come to our senses and reconnect with the (spiritual) facts of life – which constitutes an expansion of consciousness among a critical mass of humanity. World Teacher Maitreya highlights the key to ending our self-imposed cosmic confinement when he says: "The crime of separation must be driven from this world."[69] He emphasises the need to give expression to our oneness because it is our divine nature: "Man is an emerging God and thus requires the formation of modes of living which will allow this God to flourish. How can you be content with the modes within which you now live: when millions starve and die in squalor; when the rich parade their wealth before the poor; when each man is his neighbour's enemy; when no man trusts his brother? For how long must you live thus, My friends? For how long can you support this degradation?"[70]

As with the extraterrestrial presence on Earth, we have only so much room to deny the reality of the crises that our ways of organizing society have created. We have reached the end of the rope for plugging the holes, propping up the financial and economic façades of dysfunctional and all but collapsed structures that are the inheritance of humanity's long-standing refusal to accept our interconnectedness. As this chapter shows, the visitors from space have tried, time and again, from the 1950s onward, to awaken us from our slumber. If we look at the state of the world, humanity, and the planet today, it seems we are well-placed for a final wake-up call of our own making.

Chapter 2 Addendum:
The new world order is what we make it

With his own background as a business executive Stefan Denaerde, although immensely impressed by it, at first cringed at the efficiency with which society on his hosts' planet was organised: "This must be a universally governed planet, but seemingly so strictly governed that everything was streamlined and standardized. What a terrible thought!"[71] Likewise, it is often fear of uniformity or monotony that causes many people to oppose global solutions for our current problems, pointing at the terrifying threat of a New World Order that they allege the elite is trying to impose on humanity.

In my previous book I have shown how the term 'New World Order' as a label for an Orwellian society of state control, fear and oppression is a complete misnomer, given that the fast erosion of civil liberties is actually the culmination of the economic policies that started being introduced in response to the neoliberal call for 'smaller government', i.e. fewer regulations and greater freedom for corporations and markets.[72] As should now be glaringly clear, if restrictions for corporations and wealthy individuals are removed, they will use their greater freedom to secure their own interests at the expense of the rest of society by influencing not only public opinion, but also elections, the democratic process itself and the judiciary.

Not surprisingly, if we look for the origin of the term NWO, we will see that it was first used to denote the exact opposite of what fearmongers now make it out to be. After World War I, US President Woodrow Wilson argued for membership of the League of Nations, which would be crucial for a "new world order" that would transcend traditional power politics and emphasised collective security, democracy, and self-determination. When the US Senate rejected membership, the League of Nations soon fell short of its stated aims and the term "new world order" fell in disuse.

In April 1940, not long into World War II, the Tibetan Master

Djwhal Khul (DK) wrote, through Alice A. Bailey: "These two forces – materialism and spirituality – face each other. What will be the outcome? Will men arrest the evil and initiate a period of understanding, cooperation and right relationship, or will they continue the process of selfish planning and of economic and militant competition? This question must be answered by the clear thinking of the masses and by the calm and unafraid challenges of the democracies.

"On all sides the need for a new world order is being recognised. The totalitarian powers are talking of the 'new order in Europe'; the idealists and thinkers are unfolding schemes and plans which vision entirely new conditions that will bring the old bad order to an end."[73]

He explains the concepts of spirituality and materialism as follows: "Everything is spiritual which tends towards understanding, towards kindness, towards that which is productive of beauty and which can lead man on to a fuller expression of his divine potentialities. All is evil which drives man deeper into materialism, which omits the higher values of living, which endorses selfishness, which sets up barriers to the establishment of right human relations, and which feeds the spirit of separateness, of fear, of revenge."[74]

Canadian researcher Wilbert Smith at a later stage had arrived at the same insight: "The two great forces involved in trying to influence man's thinking may be described as *positive*, i.e. thoughts in harmony with the concept of a love of God and the brotherhood of man, and *negative*, those encompassing anti-Christ motives designed to gain control over man for the purpose of power. This battle for Man's mind is being waged on two fronts, the physical and the metaphysical, and the object of the fight is to bring about either the spiritual salvation or destruction of homo sapiens."[75]

Based on this distinction, the Master DK says: "The spiritual Hierarchy of the planet is throwing the weight of its strength against the [totalitarian] Axis powers just in so far as the spiritually minded peoples of the world can collaborate, for there can be no coercion of man's free will."[76] It should be clear, therefore, even to conspiracy theorists, that when, for instance, Winston Churchill spoke of a "new world order", he was not referring to a totalitarian world governing body.

In the same year, 1940, H.G. Wells published his book *The New World Order*, in which he discussed the need for a different way of organising society, in which he stated: "Either mankind collapses or our species struggles up by the hard yet fairly obvious routes I have collated in this book, to reach a new level of social organisation. There can be little question of the abundance, excitement and vigour of living that awaits our children upon that upland. If it is attained. There is no doubting their degradation and misery if it is not."[77]

Clearly, it is a sad case of manipulative 'newspeak' to label the consummation of the existing order as something that the world has been in dire need of for so long: a *new* order.

All this, of course, is not to say that there isn't a global elite whose main objective is to secure and increase its wealth, power and influence in order to perpetuate and complete their control over life on this planet as they understand it. And although there is not a shred of evidence, many people suspect an 'alien agenda' in one form or another behind this elite. If so, then 'alien' perhaps in the sense of being foreign to the human heart, not in the sense of 'extraterrestrial'. George Adamski made short work of such allegations: "With their advanced scientific knowledge which enables them to travel space, if these people [from space] were hostile could they not have conquered the world long ago? Yet, have they made the slightest move to do so?"[78] Instead, as Daniel Fry was told: "We have expended considerable time and patience in the effort to light a few candles among the many nations of your planet. It has been our hope that the light of these candles might grow in brilliance so that they will expose the terrible abyss toward which the peoples of your world are so blindly rushing."[79] "We will never attempt to force either our knowledge or our culture upon you and will never come to your people unless there is substantial evidence that they desire it."[80]

Further confirmation came from Adamski's Venusian contact Orthon: "To all of us who have from birth been instilled with the vision of the whole, it is unthinkable to disobey what we know to be the universal laws. These laws are made by no man. They were in the beginning, and will endure throughout eternity. Under these laws each individual, each group of mankind, all intelligent life on each world, must decide its own destiny without interference from another. Counsel, yes. Instruction, yes. But interference to the point of destruction, never."[81]

Adamski himself added elsewhere: "Let us remember these people are more advanced than we, and have reached that stage only by passing through and conquering the experiences we are now undergoing. They understand the struggles confronting Earthlings, therefore feel a deep compassion for us. As I have said many times, they have told me repeatedly that they only want to help us – if we will but listen and accept their help. They have no desire to hurt us, and deceit, which would naturally awaken distrust, could undo years and even centuries of their labor amongst us."[82]

In 1979 Benjamin Creme stated that contacts from space are governed by law and although less well-meaning people from other planets did come to Earth in the past, this had been stopped.[83] This is confirmed by scientist Michael Wolf who has worked alongside space people based on Earth. When researcher Paola Harris asked Wolf about "the benevolent ET/hostile ET issue" he replied: "Most are benevolent. Occasionally some get through the alien barrier, but they don't generally come back. (...) Once they have hidden agendas, once they are identified, they are barred from coming here... [The benevolent ETs] don't want negative interference..."[84]

These statements are corroborated by Wilbert Smith who, based on his own contacts, says: "[A] large number of the space brothers, whose special mission it is to safeguard the spiritual welfare and evolutional progress of Earthlings, had banded themselves together to form what might be described in Earth terms as a 'cosmic police force'. The true role of any police force, they added, is a purely defensive one – a protective measure designed to ensure the safety and well-being of society-at-large and the maintenance of law and order to safeguard this objective. (...)

"This role is mainly a dual one: (1) to keep at bay negative forces from outer space who attempt to inflict their stronger evil influence on negative and borderline-negative Earthlings; and (2) to assure that all outer space beings permitted to visit our world observe strictly the cosmic laws governing non-interference and non-hostility toward the inhabitants of planet Earth."[85]

Among those who are taking responsibility to speak out and do not need to blame some external force for what we have allowed to happen on our own planet, is Pope Francis. On his recent visit to Bolivia he condemned unbridled capitalism as "the dung of the devil", saying: "No actual or established power has the right to deprive peoples of the full exercise of their sovereignty. Whenever they do so, we see the rise of new forms of colonialism which seriously prejudice the possibility of peace and justice. The new colonialism takes on different faces. At times it appears as the anonymous influence of mammon: corporations, loan agencies, certain 'free trade' treaties, and the imposition of measures of 'austerity' which always tighten the belt of workers and the poor."[86]

To many, this might sound like a call for socialism. What we need to remember, though, is that that is merely a term, which in itself isn't bad or good, even if it reminds us of experiments with socialist societies that were (far) less than perfect for their lack of individual freedoms. As Stefan Denaerde's contacts told him: "It was a pity that the communist ideals were lost in inefficiency, otherwise they could have done a lot of good. It was a case of state-controlled economy being confused with communal ownership."[87]

However, it is good to remind ourselves here that lacking proper checks and balances the much touted capitalist system, too, is leaving the vast majority of people in the lurch, even in terms of individual freedoms in so-called 'rich' countries, as well as proving a formidable threat to our survival because of its wasteful disregard of human talents and ruthless exploitation of natural resources. Not surprisingly, Mr Denaerde's contacts were just as dismissive of the capitalist system.[88] In fact, they said, "Our cosmic universal economic system can be compared to both communism and the capitalist Western economy. One can also say that our cosmic economics can't be compared with either. (...) It is only through this system that a race can achieve a cultural level of social stability. And from there onward toward immortality. It is the cosmic condition, based on natural laws."[89]

So unless one thinks universal justice is bad, or a bad concept, it certainly is not un-democratic, un-christian, un-buddhist, un-socialist, nor even un-liberal.

George Adamski has stated that the space visitors do not support any specific form of society on Earth over another: "Such support would be complying with our custom of divisions. They recognize no false divisions of any kind. They understand Life is eternal, and every person is born to fulfill a definite destiny. Each must learn his own lessons as he travels the pathway of life. (...) Therefore, all are respected alike. So they have neither preference nor judgment for any specific form of our society."[90]

While being contacted in July 1950, Daniel Fry was told something very similar: "The political tensions which now exist between your nations must be eased. If either of the two dominant nations of earth were to achieve conclusive scientific superiority over the other, under present conditions, a war of extermination would be certain to follow. We are not here to assist any nation in making war but to stimulate a degree of progress which will eliminate the reasons for war on Earth, even as we, some thousands of years ago eliminated the reasons for conflict among our own people."[91]

Even in the midst of the Cold War George Adamski couldn't be bothered if his space contacts' view of a just society would be called 'socialist', saying: "I do not know what the word Socialism is supposed to represent. The word social means to be congenial and respect your fellow being. Jesus taught equality made up of many talents; the Space People live this Cosmic Law instead of the 'isms' that we proclaim."[92]

According to Benjamin Creme, the Masters of Wisdom "hold the view that the ideal relationship for sound social cohesion and justice is 70 per cent socialism and 30 per cent capitalism".[93] We can be certain that the Masters are not referring to the flawed systems as we have witnessed them in (recent) history, but to the original notions, which can be found at the basis of every major religion and school of thought. What's more, according to the Tibetan Master DK, at present even "true democracy is unknown, and the mass of the people in the democratic countries are as much at the mercy of the politicians and of the financial forces as are the people under the rule of dictatorships, enlightened or unenlightened."[94]

As for the aim of a more just society, the Venusian Master reassured us: "[T]here are degrees of perfection just as there are degrees of all things. In our worlds, we are happy, but we do not stagnate. Just as one reaches the top of a hill seen from below, a further hill comes into view, so it is always with progress. The valley that lies between must be crossed before the next height can be scaled."[95]

In short then, if we care to take responsibility for what happens on our planet and in our lives – inspired and guided by our Elder Brothers, the Masters of Wisdom – any new world order will be what we make it, and the Space Brothers have let us know that they can be counted on to help in as much as we will let them.

Notes

1   Stefan Denaerde (1977), *Operation Survival Earth*, p.16
2   Ibidem, p.15
3   Benjamin Creme (ed., 2011), *Share International* magazine, Vol.30, No.8, October, p.22
4   Interview with Dr Edgar Mitchell in Nick Margerrison (2008), *The Night Before*, Kerrang! Radio, UK, 23 July. Available at <www.youtube.com/watch?v=RhNdxdveK7c>
5   Enrique Barrios (1989), *Ami, Child of the Stars*, p.19
6   Ibid., p.25
7   Ibid., p.20
8   George Adamski (1957-58), *Cosmic Science for the Promotion of Cosmic Principles and Truth – Questions and Answers*, Series No.1, Part No.2, Question #40
9   Stefano Breccia (2009), *Mass Contacts*, p.172

10   Ibid., p.192
11   Maitreya, in Creme (ed.; 1992), *Messages from Maitreya the Christ*, Message No. 11, January 5, 1978
12   Adamski (1957-58), op cit, Part No.5, Question #99
13   Barrios (1989), op cit, p.100
14   Denaerde (1977), op cit, p.138
15   Barrios (1989), op cit, p.20
16   Adamski (1955), *Inside the Space Ships*, p.137
17   Daniel Fry (1954a), *A Report by Alan to Man of Earth*, as reprinted in Fry (1966), *The White Sands Incident*, p.88
18   Ibid., p.80
19   Orfeo Angelucci (1955), *The Secret of the Saucers*, p.33
20   Oxfam (2015), 'Richest 1% will own more than all the rest by 2016'. Available at <www.oxfam.org/en/pressroom/pressreleases/2015-01-19/richest-1-will-own-more-all-rest-2016> [Accessed 14 April 2015]
21   Creme (ed., 2005), *Maitreya's Teachings – The Laws of Life*, p.109
22   World Economic Forum (2014), *Outlook on the Global Agenda 2014,* Chapter 2, Widening income disparities', p.12a. Available at <www3.weforum.org/docs/WEF_GAC_GlobalAgendaOutlook_2014.pdf> [Accessed 14 April 2015]
23   Office of the Press Secretary (2014), 'President Barack Obama's State of the Union Address'. The White House [online], 28 January. Available at <www.whitehouse.gov/the-press-office/2014/01/28/president-barack-obamas-state-union-address> [Accessed 14 April 2015]
24   Adamski (1955), op cit, p.239
25   Adamski (1965a), *Cosmic Bulletin*, December 1964, p.14
26   Adamski (1957-58), op cit, Part No.2, Question #40
27   Marianne Szegedy-Maszak (2015), '71 Years Ago FDR Dropped a Truthbomb That Still Resonates Today', *Mother Jones* [online], 12 April. Available at <www.motherjones.com/kevin-drum/2015/04/fdr-roosevelt-economic-rights-national-security> [Accessed 13 April 2015]
28   'The Universal Declaration of Human Rights'. Available at <www.un.org/en/documents/udhr/>
29   Joseph A. Califano Jr. (1999), 'What Was Really Great About The Great Society – The truth behind the conservative myths'. *The Washington Monthly* [online], October. Available at <www.washingtonmonthly.com/features/1999/9910.califano.html> [Accessed 16 April 2015]
30   Denaerde (1982), *Contact from Planet Iarga*, p.91. The equivalent of this quote in the original English edition can be found on p.39 of *Operation Survival Earth*: "Culture is the measure through which a society cares to the least fortunate man. The measure in which the sick, invalid, old or poor people are taken care of. In short, the measure of collective unselfishness."
31   Adamski (1955), op cit, p.167

32 James Meek (2014), 'Sale of the century: the privatisation scam'. *The Guardian* [online], 22 August. Available at <www.theguardian.com/politics/2014/aug/22/sale-of-century-privatisation-scam> [Accessed 23 August 2014]
33 Denaerde (1977), op cit, p.50
34 Maitreya, in Creme (ed.; 1989), *Share International* magazine, Vol. 8, No.3 April, p.5
35 Buck Nelson (1956), *My Trip to Mars, the Moon and Venus*, p.16
36 Truman Bethurum (1954), *Aboard a Flying Saucer*, p.147
37 David Crary and Lisa Leff (2014), 'Number of Homeless Children in America Surges to All-Time High: Report'. *The Huffington Post* [online], 17 November. Available at <www.huffingtonpost.com/2014/11/17/child-homelessless-us_n_6169994.html> [Accessed 3 August 2015]
38 Eliza Barclay (2014), 'More cities are making it illegal to hand out food to the homeless'. NPR The Salt, 22 October [online]. Available at <www.npr.org/sections/thesalt/2014/10/22/357846415/more-cities-are-making-it-illegal-to-hand-out-food-to-the-homeless> [Accessed 8 July 2015]
39 Christopher Donato (2014), '90-Year-old man charged with feeding the homeless says he won't give up'. ABC News, 6 November [online]. Available at <abcnews.go.com/US/90-year-florida-man-charged-feeding-homeless-wont/story?id=26733223> [Accessed 8 July 2015]
40 Adamski (1957-58), op cit, Part No.5, Question #94
41 'Spain Youth Unemployment Rate'. *Trading Economics*, 14 April 2014 Available at <www.tradingeconomics.com/spain/youth-unemployment-rate>
42 Giles Tremlett (2015), 'The Podemos revolution: how a small group of radical academics changed European politics'. *The Guardian* [online], 31 March. Available at <www.theguardian.com/world/2015/mar/31/podemos-revolution-radical-academics-changed-european-politics>. [Accessed 1 April 2015]
43 Owen Jones (2014), 'It's socialism for the rich and capitalism for the rest of us in Britain'. *The Guardian* [online], 29 August. Available at <www.theguardian.com/books/2014/aug/29/socialism-for-the-rich> [Accessed 17 April 2015]
44 Amelia Gentleman (2014), ' "No one should die penniless and alone": the victims of Britain's harsh welfare sanctions'. *The Guardian*, 3 August [online]. Available at <www.theguardian.com/society/2014/aug/03/victims-britains-harsh-welfare-sanctions> [Accessed 4 August 2014]
45 Siobhan Fenton (2015), 'Welfare cuts: Statistics watchdog urges Government to release clear information on benefits sanctions'. *The Independent* [online], 8 August. Available at <www.independent.co.uk/news/uk/politics/welfare-cuts-statistics-watchdog-urges-government-

to-release-clear-information-on-benefits-sanctions-10446515.html>
[Accessed 9 August 2015]
46 Jones (2014), op cit
47 Denaerde (1977), op cit, p.42
48 Ibid., p.16
49 Ibid., p.60
50 Barrios (1989), op cit, pp.37-38
51 Ibid., p.79
52 Ibid., p.82
53 Alfie Kohn (1991), 'Caring Kids – The Role of Schools'. *Phi Delta Kappan* (March), p.497
54 Adamski (1965), *Answers to Questions Most Frequently Asked About Our Space Visitors And Other Planets*, p.17
55 Creme (2002), *The Art of Cooperation*, pp.31-32
56 Denaerde (1977), op cit, p.47
57 Wilbert Smith (1969), *The Boys from Topside*, p.30
58 Creme (2003), 'Questions and answers', *Share International* magazine, No.5, May, p.25. Official estimates ranged between eight to thirty million; see Joris Verhulst (2010), 'February 15, 2003: The World Says No to War'. In: Stefaan Walgrave & Dieter Rucht (eds.), *The world says no to war: Demonstrations against the War on Iraq*, p.1
59 Benjamin Creme's Master (1999), 'The end of the "babarian age" '. In: Creme (ed.; 2004), *A Master Speaks*, 3rd expanded edition, p.349
60 Adamski (1955), op cit, p.208
61 Ibid., p.139
62 Interview with Lachezar Filipov on BTV, Bulgaria, October 2012. Available at <www.youtube.com/watch?v=23WRbbWFBQI> [Accessed 2 March 2015]
63 Dino Kraspedon (1959), *My Contact With Flying Saucers*, p.88
64 Adamski (1955), op cit, p.90
65 Ibid., pp.116-17
66 Benjamin Creme's Master (1999), op cit.
67 Adamski (1955), op cit, p.93
68 Ibid., p.94
69 Maitreya, in Creme (ed.; 1992), op cit, Message No.93, January 22, 1980
70 Ibid., Message No.81, September 12, 1979

The new world order is what we make it
71 Denaerde (1977), op cit, p.38
72 Gerard Aartsen (2011), *Here to help: UFOs and the Space Brothers*, 2nd edition 2012, p.24ff
73 Alice A. Bailey (1957), *The Externalisation of the Hierarchy*, p.183
74 Ibid, pp.186-87

75 Smith (1969), op cit, p.30
76 Bailey (1957), op cit, p.187
77 H.G. Wells (1940), *The New World Order*, The University of Adelaide Library web edition. Available at <ebooks.adelaide.edu.au/w/wells/hg/new_world_order/index.html>
78 Adamski (1957-58), op cit, Part 1, Question #20
79 Fry (1954a), op cit, p.67
80 Fry (1954), *The White Sands Incident*, p.43
81 Adamski (1955), op cit, pp.98-99
82 Adamski (1957-58), op cit, Part No.5, Question #89
83 Creme (1979), *The Reappearance of the Christ and the Masters of Wisdom*, p.209
84 Paola Harris (2008), *Connecting the Dots... Making Sense Of The UFO Phenomenon*, p.159
85 Smith (1969), op cit, p.45
86 Reuters (2015), 'Unbridled capitalism is the "dung of the devil", says Pope Francis', *The Guardian* [online], 10 July. Available at <www.theguardian.com/world/2015/jul/10/poor-must-change-new-colonialism-of-economic-order-says-pope-francis> [Accessed 11 July 2015]
87 Denaerde (1977), op cit, p.43
88 Ibid., p.134
89 Ibid., p.39
90 Adamski (1957-58), op cit, Part 1, Question #6
91 Fry (1954), op cit, p.30
92 Adamski (1965), op cit, p.28
93 Creme (ed., 2007), 'Questions and answers'. *Share International* magazine, Vol.26, No.1, January/February, p.34
94 Bailey (1957), op cit, p.52
95 Adamski (1955), op cit, p.93

The World Teacher (pp.43-44)

a Adamski (1957-58), op cit, Part No.1, Question #10
b See Gerard Aartsen (2008), *Our Elder Brothers Return – A History in Books (1875 - Present)*, 'Various Teachings'. Published online at <www.biblioteca-ga.info/50/18>
c Giorgio Dibitonto (1990), *Angels in Starships*, pp.32-33
d Bailey (1948), *The Reappearance of the Christ*, p.69
e Adamski (1962), *Special Report : My Trip to the Twelve Counsellors' Meeting That Took Place on Saturn, March 27-30, 1962*, Part 2
f Creme (ed.), *Share International* magazine, Background information

"Their appearance is in accordance with the Universal Plan of brotherhood, wherein they offer a helping hand and words of counsel in time of need..." –George Adamski, USA

"The Space Brothers are here to help the people of Earth to overcome the difficulties which our own ignorance has brought about..." –Benjamin Creme, UK

"We derive our greatest joy from serving, helping others..." –Enrique Barrios' contact, Chile

"The governments of our world (...) have all the interest in giving the public a negative view of the extraterrestrials, who appear to be motivated, instead, by positive intentions." –Paolo di Girolamo, Italy

"They stand by ready and willing to render help. In fact, they have already helped us a great deal, along lines that do not interfere with our freedom of choice." –Wilbert Smith, Canada

"They foresee a future of great prosperity for planet Earth, if our leaders will avoid a new conflict and will confirm that they are among us, to help us." –Alberto Perego, Italy

"Decades ago, visitors from other planets warned us about where we were headed and offered to help." –Paul T. Hellyer, Canada

"They are not hostile towards us, rather, they want to help us but we have not grown enough in order to establish direct contact with them." –Prof Lachezar Filipov, Bulgaria

3. Right human relations: An extraterrestrial show-and-tell

In the face of the multitude of unfounded stories of 'alien threats' and a seemingly equal number of wishful channelings from fanciful 'galactic emissaries', the fact that there are so many testimonies of actual personal encounters which confirm that the space people are here to help humanity in this time of transition cannot be stressed and reiterated often enough (see facing page).

As for exactly *how* the space visitors are helping us, esotericist Benjamin Creme has been the most specific: "[W]hat we call the U.F.O.s (the vehicles of the space people, from the higher planets) have a very definite part to play in the building of a spiritual platform for the World Teacher, preparing humanity for this time. In fact, since the war, they have played a major role in preserving this planet intact."[1] This latter fact was also acknowledged by the Italian Consul Alberto Perego when he said: "We must be grateful to them for having prevented, until now, nuclear war."[2]

In addition, Creme continues, "The Space People release into our world tremendous cosmic energies which have a great effect in transforming humanity and in sustaining the planet as an integral being. Their work is continuous and endless, and we all owe them a tremendous debt." Elsewhere he adds: "They go through our skies mopping up and neutralizing large amounts of nuclear waste and the general toxic filth that we pour into the atmosphere." Without this, he says, "life on this planet would be very painful indeed..."

"Another part of their tremendous work for planet Earth is that they are replicating, on the physical plane, the magnetic energy field around the planet (...) in connection with a new technology which will give us unlimited, safe energy for all our needs direct from the sun: the 'science of light'..."[3] This will be put at our disposal "as soon as we renounce war forever, showing that we are able to live together in peace with justice, sharing, and right relationship."[4]

That 'right relationship' is what is missing in our systems, yet lies at the core of the view of life on the higher planets is abundantly clear when the Master from Saturn exhorts Adamski: "Never cease to point out to [those in your world] that all are brothers and sisters, regardless of where they have been born, or have chosen to live. Nationality or the color of one's skin are but incidental since the body is no more than a temporary dwelling. These change in the eternity of time. In the infinite progress of life, each eventually will know all states."[5]

Most people who are interested in the subject of UFOs and exopolitics will be aware of the descriptions of other planets in the accounts of many contactees.

#85   For instance, based on his visit to Mars, Buck Nelson said: "Mars is very colourful. I couldn't tell where one color ended and another began."[6]

The lady captain from 'Clarion' whom Truman Bethurum met several times, told him: "Mars is a beautiful place to see... There are people there, just like you and me. ... Every home has a beautiful lawn where flowers and shrubs abound..."[7] And Howard Menger describes Venus as being fantastically beauti-

Life on other planets and other planes – no 'dark' matter

When the first (contradicting) measurements of the temperature on Venus came in in 1958, George Adamski was quickly ridiculed for his statements that his contacts hailed from that and other planets in our solar system. He was not alone, though, in maintaining his claims; Dino Kraspedon (physicist-contactee Aladíno Félix), Wilbert Smith (researcher-contactee), Bruno Ghibaudi (journalist-contactee), Howard Menger (contactee) and Buck Nelson (contactee), all said, more or less publicly, that the spacecraft and their occupants come from within the solar system, mainly from Mars, Venus, Saturn and a few other planets.[a]

Since that time, though, no contactee would place the origins of the visitors from space within our own solar system. However, to this day, esotericist Benjamin Creme states categorically: "All the planets of our system are inhabited..." but, he adds, "if you were to go to Mars or Venus you would see nobody because they are in physical bodies of etheric matter."[b] Echoing Benjamin Creme's assertion that all planets are inhabited, Menger's contacts told him: "[I]f an Earth man in physical body could go there he probably would not see some of the life forms which vibrate more rapidly than his own – no more than he can see the spiritual life forms in and around his own planet. Unless his physical body were processed and conditioned, he could not see the beings on another planet."[c]

The Ageless Wisdom teaching posits the notion of four planes of matter above the dense, liquid and gaseous physical, which it calls the etheric planes of matter, each of which is made up of sub-atomic particles that vibrate at a higher frequency than those at the plane below it, and which are therefore – at our current stage in evolution – outside our range of vision. This explains how space ships can appear and disappear at will. It was, again, George Adamski who was closest to the mark in this respect, when he said: "[A]ll Nature is etheric; whether in a form or formless state. (...) [W]hen the word 'ether' is properly understood, you can see it has no reference to spirits or disembodied entities."[d] And about the space visitors: "[T]hey can place their mind in a high frequency state that causes their body to become invisible to our limited range of vision."[e]

According to Benjamin Creme, since the space ships consist of etheric physical matter, whose rate of vibration for the purpose of sightings may be lowered into the dense physical frequency, one can only enter a space ship in the etheric body, i.e. one's conscious awareness has to be 'lifted' from the dense physical body into the etheric body. In *Here to Help: UFOs and the Space Brothers* I presented tacit evidence to this fact from several contactees who testified to a heightened state of awareness once they were on a ship.[f] A possible description of the process of being taken out of the (dense physical) body comes from Howard Menger, whose hosts explained: "We projected the beam on you to condition and process your body quickly so you could enter the craft. What actually happened was that the beam changed your body frequency to equal that of the craft."[g]

Anyone who thinks this is far-fetched would do well to remember that, based on astrophysical calculations about the mass of the universe, science itself admits it doesn't understand what 96 per cent of the known universe consists of and since the 1930s calls 'dark matter'. Since that time, though, several trailblazing scientists have made discoveries which all point in the same direction as (partial) explanations for or proof of 'dark matter', aka the etheric planes of matter.

Reiterating briefly: Semyon Kirlian developed a technique to record the otherwise invisible energy fields emanating from living organisms; Wilhelm Reich MD discovered a primordial life force that permeates everything, which he called 'orgone', and Rupert Sheldrake has shown through experiments the existence of morphogenetic fields from which nature's blueprints precipitate into the life forms as we know them.[h]

In March 2015 these 'avant garde' ideas almost stealthily gained confirmation when mainstream science reported findings which "suggest that dark matter is another kind of sub-atomic particle, possibly forming a parallel universe of 'supersymmetry' filled with super-symmetrical matter that behaves like an invisible mirror-image of ordinary matter."[i] Therefore, when we read scientific assertions that there is no life on the other planets in our solar system, we just need to add "...on the dense physical planes of matter." *Notes on page 125*

ful: "I did not get the impression of cities; instead, I was reminded of beautiful suburban areas I have seen on our own planet, though, of course, wonderously different. The buildings were set in natural surroundings with large trees, which looked something like our redwoods, and gardens stretching in every direction. Then I saw forests, streams, large bodies of water. People, dressed in soft pastel colors moved about. I also saw four-legged animals which were unfamiliar to me."[8] He later adds: "They live in small communities, built in the forests and close to natural surroundings. They do not denude the lands of all trees and shrubs and then build boxes. Their communities are kept small..."[9]

George Adamski wrote: "Although they have innumerable central communities, they do not have gigantic, congested cities as we do on Earth. For while we use only a relatively small portion of our total land, they utilize the soil of their entire planet for the needs of the people. They do not bleed the land of its fertility as we do, but practice rotation of crops, and return to the earth a certain percentage of nature's produce for mulching and fertilizing. All land is given periodic rest. Cooperating with Nature as they do, they find the use of poison sprays, artificial fertilizers, etc., unnecessary. (...) They know that all life-forms are important in the Cosmic Plan, and without human interference Nature provides amply for all her children, yet maintains an eternal equilibrium."[10]

Like Howard Menger, Adamski observed: "All cities followed a circular or oval pattern, and none appeared in any way congested. Between these concentrated communities there was much still uninhabited territory. (...) The streets were well laid out and beautifully bordered with flowers of many colors."[11] Likewise, "the farmhouses were not scattered around the countryside, but also followed a circular plan. I was told that this arrangement had been found more practical in enabling these farm groups to become small, self-sufficient communities, containing everything necessary to supply all commodities for the country folk."[12]

On 'Iarga', all areas suitable for habitation have housing complexes that also follow a circular pattern, according to the description of Stefan Denaerde, whose account includes several detailed drawings based on his information. His contacts told him: "[W]e call them house rings because they are in fact built in the form of a ring with a covered central recreation area."[13]

Adamski continues his description of life on Venus as follows: "In their community way of life, with respect toward one another and with life's necessities provided for all, they find no need for penal institutions with their associate personnel. Because the people on Venus, Mars and elsewhere in our system have learned to live harmoniously with one another, they have no tensions and consequently no sickness. (...)

"They have no need for medicines because they receive the necessary bodily requirements from their food. In case of an accident, their understanding of the human body enables them to assist one another. Considering all this, it is understandable why they have no need for doctors, nurses or hospitals." This way of living, he continues, is also possible on Earth: "The prime requisite is that each individual learn to be harmonious within himself, and in association with others."[14]

While many at present might find Buck Nelson's enthusiasm for a teetotal society somewhat premature or unappealing, it is clear that he confirms Adamski's information when he says: "[T]he people of the other planets in our solar system are able to live in an order without wars; without armed forces or police; without tobacco, coffee or tea; without liquor and harmful drugs; from the use of unrefined natural foods, disease is very

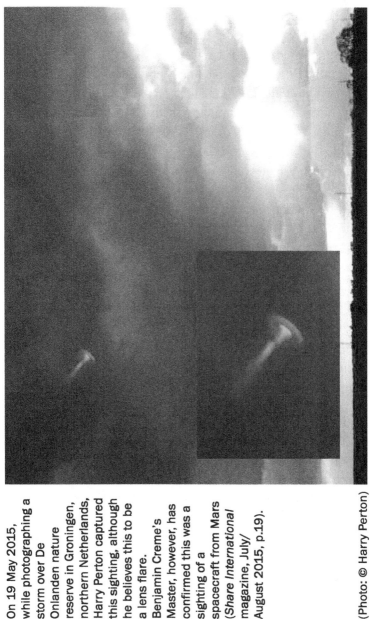

On 19 May 2015, while photographing a storm over De Onlanden nature reserve in Groningen, northern Netherlands, Harry Perton captured this sighting, although he believes this to be a lens flare. Benjamin Creme's Master, however, has confirmed this was a sighting of a spacecraft from Mars (*Share International* magazine, July/August 2015, p.19).

(Photo: © Harry Perton)

rare, hence no hospitals, no prisons or sanitariums. The span of life is greatly extended, the cost of government is very small, the rule being based on truth and justice."[15] To which he adds: "The government of these people on other planets seems to be very simple. They called it 'home life'. Actually living according to the Golden Rule (...) eliminates the need for great government buildings, munitions, armies, police forces and jails."[16]

This, in turn, is corroborated by Howard Menger, who writes: "They do not have authorities or government officials of any kind. They live in peace and harmony and everyone knows what his or her particular talent is so that they work at that particular job – and they love their work."[17]

Truman Bethurum's contact said: "The things that trouble and worry you earth people ... in our homes you'll never find. We know nothing of illness, doctors or nurses."[18] "Other planets are much too busy improving the welfare of their inhabitants to have time for even minor controversies."[19] Mr Bethurum himself added: "I also got the impression that cooperation among all of their people is an inherent feature of their lives, and that poverty is unknown. Also, that what we call riches or wealth is certainly more evenly distributed than on our earth. That their people are very busy living and learning, and not worrying what someone else has or does not have."[20]

Buck Nelson had a very similar observation: "Folks on Mars, the Moon and Venus look like us here on Earth, but they are much better looking in general. (...) They ate some meat. At least what I had looked and tasted like meat. Their food seemed to consist mainly of fruits and vegetables. They were healthy, happy people. I was told that disease is rare..."[21] Likewise, Howard Menger's contact told him: "On my planet sickness is a rare occurrence: but when a body does show symptoms of some ailment, this same body realizes it has been negligent in

A somewhat similar sighting as that on p.89 appears in this photograph of the aurora borealis in Andenes, northern Norway, 20 January 2010.
(Photo: © Per-Arne Mikalsen, Andenes, Norway)

living one of our Infinite Father's natural laws."[22]

This direct connection between a just economic system based on free access to the necessities of life and our physical health was already pointed out in the 1940s when the Tibetan Master Djwhal Khul wrote: "The keynote to good health, esoterically speaking, is sharing or distribution, just as it is the keynote to the general well-being of humanity. The economic ills of mankind closely correspond to disease in the individual. There is lack of a free flow of the necessities of life to the points of distribution; these points of distribution are idle: the direction of the distribution is faulty, and only through a sane and worldwide grasp of the New Age principle of sharing will human ills be cured..."[23]

As we saw in the previous chapter, the space visitors have shared their deep insight in what causes our problems on Earth at this time, but far less well-known is the fact that they have also been showing us alternatives for the broken systems that we have been putting up with for decades. George Adamski, in particular, has been ridiculed for his descriptions of life on Venus and the spiritual world view underlying it, but many more details have been made available by Stefan Denaerde about how society on their planets is organised.

Although a few authors have addressed this aspect of the information coming from the contactees before, they are mainly debunkers who equate the contactees' stories with a new religion, or – correctly – link it to the wisdom teachings coming from H.P. Blavatsky and Alice A. Bailey, and therefore dismiss

Page 93: Another similar craft was captured in July 1957 by Mrs William Felton Barrett of Massachusetts, USA while on a cruise in Norway. She stated she had not seen anythying while taking the photograph, but that the craft appeared when the picture was developed and printed.

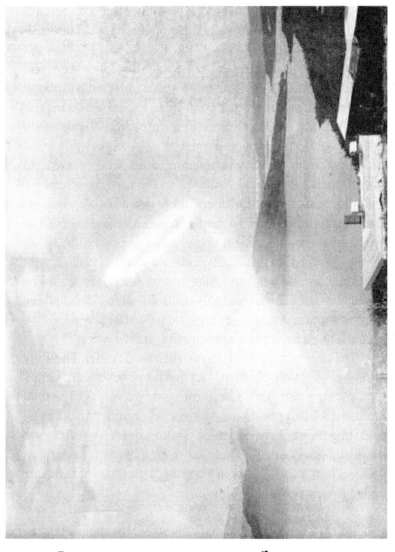

This photograph was first published in *Flying Saucer Review*, Vol.4, No.6, November-December 1958 and later used for the cover of the first English edition of Dino Kraspedon's book *My Contact With Flying Saucers* (1959).

these stories, obviously not hindered by much understanding of either the teaching or the urgency and relevance of the information for today's world.

However, it is nothing short of astounding to see the extent to which Adamski's en Denaerde's statements find corroboration in the accounts of other contactees, showing us what our Space Brothers see as priorities to restore sanity to our world and salvage it for our own future.

Based on his two-day interaction with a saucer crew from 'Iarga', Stefan Denaerde summarized the need for global cooperation and true freedom for people – instead of corporations – to ensure that the basic needs of everyone are met: "The universal economic system shows itself in practice to be an efficient production system of goods and services, placing prior importance in the sectors housing, nutrition and transport. The produce is then shared by simply controlling the individual use or consumption. The aim of this system is to free the individual as much as possible from non-creative, servile work."[24]

"The beginning of this system is their world order. The unity of such a race comes from the fact that they obey a set of Godly laws and therefore have a uniform legal system. (…) The total production of all goods and services is controlled by globally operating trusts or cooperatives, the presidents of which form the world-government. These are not so much economic as political formations that perform most of the tasks that fall here under governments and ministeries."[25]

Readers will have noticed that contactees, or their contacts, can often be found speaking in terms of God, the Creator, the Father, et cetera. While we may have good reason to question the sincerity of organised religions, and certainly the morality of individual members of the clergy of most, it should be clear that the Space Brothers invariably speak from a profound understanding and inner experience of the reality which we on Earth only know through the agency of our Teachers. For a proper appraisal of such statements it would therefore be helpful to differentiate between the Teachers and their teaching on the one hand, and those who have acted as intermediaries or interpreters, whether their aim was to further their own selfish agenda or not, on the other.

George Adamski's contacts repeatedly pointed out what the space visitors mean by 'Godly laws': "In both the old and new Testaments of the Christian Bible, and in the teachings of all the Great Ones, we find the commandment of Love. 'Love thy neighbor as thyself.' To fully understand the true meaning of this commandment we must broaden our concept of the word 'neighbor'. Neighbor is not just the person living next door, but everyone in the world; everyone living on the other planets in our system; every one living in the vast, limitless Cosmos."[26] As Adamski explains, the space visitors are so far ahead of us because "millions of years ago the people on other planets in our system began respecting one another as brothers and sisters of one planetary family, recognizing all as children of the one Infinite Creator."[27]

In his booklet *My Trip to Mars, the Moon and Venus*, Buck Nelson commented: "They really live by the laws of God"[28], while Enrique Barrios' protagonist Ami tells his young Earth friend Pete: "We don't make war because we really do believe in God."[29] As the Master from Venus told Adamski: "You have been told that in our worlds we *live* the Creator's laws, while as yet on Earth you only talk of them. If you would *live* by the precepts of even what you now know, the peoples of Earth would not go out to slaughter one another. They would work within themselves, their own groups, their own nations, to achieve good and happiness in that section of your world wherein they were born and therefore call 'home.' "[30] And elsewhere a contact from Saturn tells him: "You have set aside a day each year for the observance of the Brotherhood of Man, and you speak of the Fatherhood of the Creator. Yet, in complete oblivion of the actions which such declarations should bring forth, you lavish money and effort toward swifter and more widespread ways of maiming and destroying your fellow men on Earth. Does it not seem curious to pray to the Divine Father to bless your efforts in this ruthless destruction?"[31]

Stefan Denaerde's contacts were not reluctant to refer to Christ's teachings either when they explained how humanity might enter the higher regions of evolution: "The first [law of cosmic selection] confirms Christ's condemnation of social discrimination. A high level of technical development liquidates every discrimination and compulsion under pain of chaos and eventual self-destruction. The Earth demonstrates the justice of this law in a convincing manner. The social chaos exists already and the threat begins to manifest itself. At the moment only the great powers have nuclear weapons at their disposal, but the smaller nationalist groups will soon be in the same position. The situation becomes more dangerous every year. Within a short time you will discover the possibility of immaterial radiation [the neutron bomb? GA] and then a handful of people will be capable of producing a weapon that is capable of destroying all mankind. Where does all this lead? How long can a civilization continue to exist where science does not know its responsibilities?"

"The second law compels the correct understanding of human relationships. It poses 'Christian love' as a condition for cosmic integration. Only unselfish behaviour that restores original efficiency of natural order can give an intelligent race the certainty of survival until cosmic integration is achieved."[32]

In contrast, "[a] race that lives under the constant threat of war and destruction does not logically make any plans for the distant future" and hence will not be properly concerned with creating and maintaining planetary conditions for long-term survival. Therefore, "[t]he Earth (...) lives for the present and the past, and does not worry about the future generations."[33]

On his encounter with visitors from space at White Sands, New Mexico, USA, where the first atom bombs were tested in the 1940s, Daniel Fry, too, was told: "With the lessons of the past constantly before our people, we have found it wise to always maintain the material values in proper relationship with the more important social and spiritual values."[34] In fact, his contacts confirmed: "When the industries of your nations are released from the necessity of expending their time and energy to produce the means of war and destruction, they will then have the time and the energy to raise the standards of living of everyone on your earth to a point where there would be complete freedom from want. With freedom from want comes freedom of fear and your civilization would be safely past the critical point in its development."[35]

Some thirty-five years ago, this notion was embraced by the Independent Commission on International Development Issues, a large group of former world leaders and other prominent figures covering the full political spectrum from the left to the right under the chairmanship of former West German Chancellor Willy Brandt. In his foreword to the Commission's 1980 report, *North-South – A Programme for Survival*, Mr Brandt wrote: "At the beginning of a new decade, only twenty years short of the millennium, we must try to lift ourselves above the day-to-day quarrels (or negotiations) to see the menacing long-term problems. We see a world in which poverty and hunger still prevail in many huge regions; in which resources are squandered without consideration of their renewal; in which more armaments are made and sold than ever before; and where a destructive capacity has been accumulated to blow up our planet several times over."[36] Insightful as this assessment of the state of the world was in 1980, it is even more valid today.

It should therefore not surprise us that one of the Masters of Wisdom who Benjamin Creme says will be working openly in the world alongside the World Teacher outlined a to-do list for humanity along very similar lines: "To aid men in their task, [the World Teacher] has formulated certain priorities which (…) are simple and self-evident, yet nowhere do they exist to any great extent. Enumerated, they cover the essential needs of every man, woman and child: the first priority is an adequate supply of the right food. Secondly, adequate housing and shelter for all. Thirdly, healthcare and education as a universal right. These are the minimum requirements for a stabilized world and will become the main responsibilities of governments everywhere to ensure. Simple as they are, their inauguration will have far-reaching effects, and will usher in a new era for this Earth."[37]

While politicians often denounce people from Asia, Africa and Latin America who are seeking a better future in other parts of the world as 'fortune seekers' or 'economic refugees', the Universal Declaration of Human Rights does not make any distinction between political, religious, social or economic oppression. As Article 25 states: "Everyone has the right to a standard of living adequate for the health and well-being of himself and of his family, including food, clothing, housing and medical care and necessary social services, and the right to security in the event of unemployment, sickness, disability, widowhood, old age or other lack of livelihood in circumstances beyond his control."[38]

Long before the massive migration from regions ravaged by war or economic injustice that we now see reported in the news every day, in 2001 Benjamin Creme asked: "Do we really imagine that the people of the developing world will put up with this state of affairs for ever? Do we think they do not know what is actually taking place, what other people have, how they live, the waste? They are beginning to demand their rights."[39]

So how do we get from the present system steeped in injustice and bondage to a new reality of justice and freedom?

On Venus, Adamski tells us, "[t]heirs is a planetary government composed of a body of representatives elected from every district and every walk of life. The needs of the people are considered impartially by this body, and problems are solved for the common good of all. It is my understanding, there is very little need for legislative control. For with full recognition and adequate recompense for work well done, temptations that a monetary system such as ours presents are completely eliminated."[40] Also, "there is true equality in all respects, including allocation of commodities."[41]

In response to questions about the means of exchange on other planets, George Adamski wrote in October 1957: "Their means of exchange is a commodity and service exchange system, without the use of money. All production is for the benefit of everyone, with each receiving according to their needs. And since no money is involved, there are no 'rich'; there are no 'poor'. But all share equally, working for the common good."[42]

Likewise, says Stefan Denaerde, on 'Iarga', "[n]othing is paid for (...), only registered. What a consumer uses is registered in the computer center in each of the house cylinders, and this may not exceed that to which he has a right. These computers are coupled to the huge shopping centers in each of the cylinders. You cannot buy anything. Large and expensive things, such as houses, cars, boats, valuable artifacts, and so on, can only be hired. They call this the right of acquisition. Less expensive things are not hired because that is not efficient. They are registered for their total value and the right of use remains for life. This is almost the same as personal ownership, except that in the event of death, the goods are returned to the [production] trusts." For consumption and public services, "[t]heir total value is registered, at which point right of usage becomes yours. (…) It is practically the same sort of thing as a bank account, except that they place the control on the expenditure, whereas we place it on the income."[43]

Esotericist and futurologist Benjamin Creme has foretold an advanced system of barter as the means of distributing resources after the economic meltdown that is about to hit humanity, and it is interesting to find hints to a similar system in the accounts of several contactees about life on other planets.

Just as Stefan Denaerde was asked to leave people free to believe his story or not (see page 7), George Adamski, too, was asked to merely share the information he was given by his space contacts without trying to convince anyone – which apparently he could have if he had been allowed to tell everything he knew, as one of his close associates once told Desmond Leslie.[44] In a similar fashion, Chilean author Enrique Barrios was asked to write about the experience he had in 1985 as if it were a children's story. In his book *Ami, Child of the Stars*, he uses an inspiring and uplifting exchange between his protagonists Ami, the visitor from space, and Pete, the Earth boy who is contacted, to present his readers with information about life on other planets. In a series of discussions he humorously clarifies how much our thinking centres around the notion of possession and the need to earn money. Barrios names Ami's home planet 'Ophir', which has Biblical connotations of wealth: "Here everything belongs to all...,"[45] Ami explains to Pete, while on Earth 'progress' is measured in the personal accumulation of wealth or possessions.

Ami: "Here money doesn't exist..."

Pete: "Then how do they buy?"

Ami: "They don't buy. If they need something, they go and take it..."

Pete: "Anything?"

Ami: "Whatever they need."

Pete: "Anything at all?"

Ami: "If someone needs it, and it's available, why not? (...) everything belongs to everyone, to whoever needs it, while they are using it."[46]

When the two friends are back on Earth and they spot some UFOs over nectarine groves in Pete's village, Ami says "The appearance of UFOs is frequent in the nectarine groves of Earth", to which Pete asks: "You steal them?"

Ami: "Steal ... what is to steal?"...

Pete: "To take what belongs to another."

Ami: "Oh, *belonging* again. I guess we just can't help the 'bad customs' of our planets," he laughed. He observes that people on Earth "can't give if they are not going to receive, in return" which brings Pete to muse that "Ami had a very special way of saying hard things, always with a smile." Pete then expresses his concern about people taking advantage of others, for instance if a man would come with a truck to take all his fruit. Ami explains: "In a civilized society no one 'takes advantage of anyone.' What will that man do with the truck full of fruit?" Replies Pete: "Sell it of course...", instantly reminding readers how conditioned we are to think in terms of monetary value when we remember just a split-second later, as does Pete, that there is no money, and therefore no profit motive, in a civilized world.[47]

For a stable society, Stefan Denaerde learns, "There are only two solutions: everyone must own the same; or no one must own anything. The last one is the most efficient."[48] The efficiency of this kind of justice is "an economic plan, aimed at efficiently satisfying man's needs so that he is released from the tyranny of material things over his daily life. In other words, if everyone has everything at his disposal, then the acquisition of material goods is no longer of paramount importance. This can only be achieved by providing equal shares for everyone; otherwise envy will always exist. The culture then becomes less stable."[49]

On his trip to Venus, Howard Menger finds out: "There is no work as we know it. They have advanced mechanics and apparatus that do the work quickly and efficiently. All services are voluntary and rendered with love. All products are shared."[50] Yet, "[t]here are buildings where work is done, or where the craft are built; but the buildings are beautiful places and not like our factories at all. They receive no coin in exchange for work. Instead they exchange talents, and everything is shared to the extent of their talents and desires and no one wants for anything. We work because we have to work. They work in service of their Infinite Father."[51] Similarly, Stefan Denaerde is told: "The universal economic system that exists by a great many intelligent races, does not concern itself with money, possession, or payment. The aim of this system is to free the people from material influences and motivation..."[52]

However, based on the information that Mr Denaerde is given, this is not deemed realistic in the early stages of the transition into an economic system based on justice, and interestingly his contacts offer some practical tips to smoothen such a transition: "The goal of the universal economic system is naturally the leveling of income, but that is not possible in the early stages of social stability. A material reward must be offered to stimulate a greater personal effort. A similar reward must also be offered to stimulate young people to complete the long studies necessary to reach high technological development, or to induce people to work harder or to accept more responsibility."[53]

That the space people's social norms are well ahead of ours is also evident from their views on women's rights: "You must begin by determining a social minimum that everyone always receives and you must attempt to establish security for everyone, young and old. Women also have a right to their own income; the social minimum must be free of any discrimination. You must also determine that the maximum and the combined income for a man and wife can never exceed four times the determined minimum."[54] "We have told you that we no longer have any class distinctions, and this also applies to women. Chores are shared equally by everyone."[55]

"Iargan men and women are equals, but have different mandates. Women have the dominant position because they must lead the mental development, they are not sex objects. The subject of sex, which here on Earth is regarded as forbidden fruit and therefore takes on an unhealthy appeal, has no adverse effect on us at all. A man-woman relationship that is based solely on sex we consider degrading. Our women would rather die on the spot than be used for a kind of physical [exercise]; they make high demands of their partners. They demand their interest, their tenderness and mostly their respect for her as a person, for her intellectual level. Everything is directed at creative expression and the sex act plays a very minor part in it."[56]

We should remember that these statements were made in around 1965, when in 2015 women in most wealthy nations are still not even remunerated at the same level as men for the same job, and the debate about a universal basic income is only just beginning to gain traction in some parts of the world.

As these descriptions indicate, the only way out of our problems on Earth is the recognition of our mutual interdependence and the need for international policies to ensure that the basic needs of every human being are met. While the people on Earth at present are caught in a grossly skewed system that reduces them to servants of 'the economy' and where austerity measures that cut deep into social services are justified by politicians as "necessary to stimulate the economy", the strictly regulated economic system on 'Iarga' instead serves the needs of the people and even helps Mr Denaerde to see how a system based on justice also helps freedom to flourish when he "had begun to notice the wonderful perfection of this strange world; a world that sustained its huge population through utmost efficiency; a world without refuse, smells, exhaust gases, traffic jams and noise."[57]

If we are genuinely concerned with the well-being of every human being, it is not difficult to see that solving the problems of hunger and poverty on Earth and the related problems of scarcity of raw materials, environmental degradation and climate change, even now, is not a question of increased production of food, raw materials, medicines, know-how et cetera, but merely a matter of sharing, equal redistribution across the globe. Hence, in order to address such massive global issues, a global approach is essential.

Stefan Denaerde was shown how this is organised on 'Iarga' in unprecedented detail: "The total production of goods and services is, on Iarga, in the hands of a very small number of huge companies, the 'trusts.' These are huge organizations with millions of employees, active over their whole planet. There are primary trusts, which distribute directly to the consumer, and secondary trusts, which supply the primary."[58]

"[A]ll the goods remain the property of the trusts that supplied them. This means not only that the trust is responsible for the upkeep, repair and the guarantee of a certain minimum life, but they also take the total risk of loss or destruction. Thus, all the articles are made to such a high standard that repair is never necessary; repairs are not only expensive but terribly inefficient."[59]

Generally, "[t]he trusts work on a cost price basis whereby our term 'profit' is replaced by 'the cost of continuation.' Each trust was constantly occupied with improving and expanding its production. Their economy was as stable as a rock."[60] However, there are also scarce articles, presumably luxury items, that represent a profit far above the cost price: "Trusts absorb this extra profit and use it to subsidize other articles in the production scheme. Careful central planning can also influence the law of supply and demand."[61]

"The system worked with divisions and branches that were as far removed from one another, geographically, as possible, and allowed for automatic production. At the head of each trust was a president who was a member of the production group of the world government. (...) Their cost price was computed on the standard work hour, the *ura*."[62]

"The presidents of the two trusts are a part of the central planning group of the world government. This group attempts to lead the race to the goal of a culture. To begin with, they must, by means of production adjustment, dispense with the law of supply and demand, and thereafter create a situation of un-bridled prosperity, so that no one is troubled any more by material things. As a result this group also stimulates the mental development of the race. Take, for example, the cars and houses. There comes a time when the cultural level has reached a point where these no longer function as status symbols. What then influences the choice of the public? Two things, mainly: comfort and price. Maximum comfort and low production cost can only be achieved with robot automation. And what happens then? Everyone chooses the most efficient car and the most efficient house and so the development proceeds."[63]

Once the law of supply and demand is abolished, "[c]ompetition exists only through the free choice of the consumers, and has nothing to do with trying to influence that choice, as we try to do with advertising."[64]

Stefan Denaerde explains that on 'Iarga' there are also two worldwide consumer organizations that "are responsible for all market research. They examine the usage value of all the goods and services and inform the public in the most objective manner about the available assortment. They stimulate the trusts to produce the goods that are needed. The trusts are not permitted to advertise or exert any influence on the consumer, as this could never be objective. Thus the choice is not made by inexpert or [price-unconscious] persons but by experts with test facilities at their disposal. When, for example, they see that it is necessary that the public have a choice of five different types of television sets, then they ensure that these are produced."[65]

He continues: "The consumers cooperations comment on the performance of the trusts and so stimulate the assortment and availability. Once this situation has been reached, there is not much left to be written in a book on economics. The only thing that could be entered is any idea to improve the system's product efficiency which will reduce the amount of servile labor."[66]

Since personal ownership does not exist, natural resources are free in principle. "This meant that the price was calculated from the cost of winning, processing and distribution."[67] His contacts told him: "What we conveniently call 'price' is in fact purely a method of expressing the production time demanded by a certain article, and is only used to determine the distribution of prosperity. When you ask if the prices are high, you really mean to ask if there is a lot available to us, if we are rich or poor. In fact you are asking about the production level per head of the population, and compared to Earth's standards, this is very high. The answer is, we are all rich."[68]

Hence, on 'Iarga' there are no upper or lower classes, "only a difference between directive and executive work. When we talk about a short work period, we are talking about noncreative production and maintenance work, and everyone does this, even the president. Direction is purely creative work and we do this in our free time. (…) We do not differentiate between high and low positions. We choose people to direct us who, outside of their slave [i.e. workaday] labor, also have an interest in this activity as an expression of their creativity, like a hobby. In this stage of development, creativity is no longer considered labor, because it is the target of men."[69]

Enrique Barrios, too, is told that on 'Ophir', "[t]here is very little work, as you know it, to do. Computers have taken up all the tasks on this planet."[70] When Pete asks his extraterrestrial friend how many hours per day people work there, Ami explains: "It depends on the type of work. If it is pleasant they work a full day, like I'm doing at the moment … but this is a great privilege." Pete then asks: "You are working? What are you working on? … It seems to me we are cruising around…" Says Ami: "I am something like a professor or messenger, it's almost the same thing."[71] Elsewhere Ami said that on his planet people "live, work, study, enjoy, serve, help who they can, but since in our worlds there are no major problems, we help the uncivilized worlds…"[72] For, as Adamski's contact Orthon told him, "The conception of 'We are our brother's keeper' applies to all mankind everywhere."[73] Indeed, says the Master from

Saturn: "...all forms, by serving willingly, grow in understanding of the source from which they receive their wisdom: the same life-force by which they exist."[74]

So it appears it is service that drives the evolution towards the 'super-culture' or 'cosmic civilization' that Denaerde's hosts repeatedly refer to, and that has been lacking in the way we relate to each other on Earth. Yet, it is a process of evolution and the other planets have progressed along this path further than we have, as George Adamski explains: "Our space friends have tried to awaken us to the reality of our own misguided thinking; they can understand us, for they too have had to discipline their minds, and divert the individual ego into channels of service for others. They are interested in accomplishment, not for themselves, but for the betterment of all."[75]

In the words of the Venusian Master: "On our planet, and on other planets within our system, the form which you call 'man' has grown and advanced intellectually and socially through various stages of development to a point which is inconceivable to the people of your Earth. This development has been accomplished only by adhering to what you would term the laws of Nature. In our worlds it is known as growth through following the laws of the All Supreme Intelligence which governs all time and space."[76]

This important aspect is clearly missing from our understanding of Life, so let us explore a little further what the visitors from space have to say about it. The Master from Saturn, for instance, explained that "man himself has brought about the desolation which he so bitterly deplores, all because of service not rendered as it is naturally rendered by the humbler forms that surround him."[77] Firkon reassured Adamski, however: "The goal lost yesterday can be won tomorrow. This does not mean that we believe ourselves developed to the fullest extent.

Far from it. We have eternity yet to travel. But on our worlds, we no longer have sickness or poverty, as you know it; nor crime as you know it."[78]

Interestingly, after Stefan Denaerde had made the acquaintance of his hosts by rescuing one of them, he wondered if it hadn't just been a means to establish contact and if his help had actually been necessary. The reply was revealing in itself: "The value of an unselfish deed cannot in any way be influenced by asking afterwards if it could not have been done in some other way."[79] Elsewhere his hosts left him in no doubt about exactly how crucial this quality is for the progress of mankind: "Unselfishness makes an intelligent race immortal."[80]

As Enrique Barrios has Ami explain: "If there is love in you, you will be happy to serve others, and that way you will also have the right to be served ... you can go to your neighbor's and take from his crops what you need; from the milkman you take milk, from the baker bread, and so on. And instead of doing everything in an isolated, disorganized way, society organizes itself and takes the products to the distribution centers, and if, instead of working *yourself*, technology does it for you..." To which Pete exclaims: "No one will *do* anything!" But Ami replies: "There is always something to do. What is better than free time?"[81]

American contactee Buck Nelson wrote in 1956 that when he began to see the connection between the advantages of a more advanced civilization, which doesn't need a police force, jails or government buildings, as he observed on Venus, "and the fact that the things they use are built to last forever, so much longer than ours, and that sickness is almost unknown, then it wasn't so hard to understand why they work only about an hour a day and never more than three hours. Even housework, the spaceman told me, requires no more than one to three hours.

This leaves plenty of leisure time for visiting and they do plenty of that."[82]

When Ami tells his friend Pete that on 'Ophir' people enjoy the most complete freedom, Pete asks him if there are no laws. To which Ami replies: "Yes there are, but they are all based on the Fundamental Law of the Universe, on the good of all people."[83]

It took Stefan Denaerde some time to understand his hosts' emphasis on the need for justice: "Although I had only just begun to become acquainted with this distant culture, I understood that everyone here had equal rights. They lived in the same houses, rode in the same cars and stepped into the same trains. There were neither rich nor poor; there was no separation between nationalities, races or colors."[84] They explained to him: "What we needed to create a high level of culture were three things: freedom, justice and efficiency. (...) You are shocked by our efficiency. To us, it is the most normal thing in the world, because without this concept, we simply could not exist. Without efficiency, our world would immediately collapse. You will continually come up against this concept in our explanations because we must make it clear to you how carefully each of the three concepts – freedom, justice and efficiency – we had to employ to reach the level of civilization that can be called stable."[85]

When we look at the proposals that were put forward by the Brandt Commission in their 1980 report, we can see how much justice and efficiency are lacking on Earth: an emergency aid programme to assist countries on the verge of disaster; debt forgiveness; fair trade arrangements; stabilization of world currencies; reduction in the arms trade; global responsibility of the environment; and a major overhaul of the global economic system.

Also, Mr Denaerde's hosts explain, "justice is a condition

for efficiency. For example, if houses play a part in showing a difference in status between people, then justice fails, and efficiency in a setting such as this is impossible. It demands, therefore, a different, more social way of life."[86]

In order to secure such commitment to a viable future, Mr Denaerde hears: "All Iargans have the same duty to the children in the group in which they live. The upbringing of the child to the mentally stable and developed adult that a high culture needs is a difficult and complicated task. The schools plant the knowledge by means of the radiation but the adults must help the child to transform this knowledge into experience. The home sphere plays an important part in the development of these things. A race that seeks income levelling must give the utmost attention to raising the mental level of the people, because the raising of the general minimum wage must be in balance with this level. Value and income differences between people can be overcome only by a high minimum mental level."[87]

Denaerde explains: "The means of teaching was exactly the same as was used for me in the spaceship: a film with a simple explanation; the real information was transmitted by the radiation. (…) This basic schooling continued until the child had reached the age of fifteen or sixteen years. When I think of the information that I gained in two days from the radiation, I can imagine the level these children must reach when subjected to the radiation for ten years or more. Their basic schooling must be above the level of our universities. Having completed this basic instruction, the children moved on to the advanced schools, a normal cylinder where all the students lived together and where they could specialize in their chosen subjects."[88]

"Only when man is free of material influences can he succeed in bringing up children who, through their unselfish mental attitude, can be really free and happy. You must teach them to love and concern themselves with others. They must learn to be very expressive with their feelings. This makes great demands on their eloquence, to be able to put their feelings into words. This is characterized by their honesty, spontaneity and enthusiasm, their helpfulness and, above all, their ability to raise their love contacts above the physical to great spiritual heights. We seek adventure in the quantity and depth of our human contacts."[89]

"Happiness and satisfaction means reaching the goal of your creativeness together with others, as long as this strengthens the feeling of self-respect."[90] "Everyone who fulfils his or her task with interest and inventiveness feels happy. What more could one possibly expect from life than being successful in love and able to teach this to children."[91]

Here too, others have been imparted very similar notions. Enrique Barrios, for instance is told: "The purpose of life is to be happy, to enjoy it, but the greatest happiness comes from serving others…"[92] And George Adamski learnt: "Life is more joyous [on the other planets], for all are working and living for the common good."[93]

He later elaborated: "Every person is born to fulfill a destiny. Under our present system, even though our inner desires may yearn toward other goals, our first consideration must be making a living to meet our daily needs. Since no man exists without these deep-seated aspirations, could the limitations now placed upon him by circumstances be alleviated, he would be able to pursue them naturally for the betterment of himself and all mankind.

"I have been told degrees of intellectuality on our neighboring planets, are comparable to those on Earth. There are the laborers, the scientists, the farmers, and so on. All are necessary for a well-balanced civilization, so all are respected equally;

because they play their essential roles in solving the problems of the planet. It is their custom to work only a few hours per week, devoting the remainder of their time to study, recreation, and travel. Not only do they travel extensively throughout their own world, but to other planets in our system and sometimes to those beyond. (...) Would such a way of life be insipid? Would it not give us the leisure to unfold our natural talents, rather than stifle them? Remember, where there is interest, you will always find incentive toward something finer. The boredom which most Earthlings fear, is the result of mental immaturity. These people will experience it, regardless of how many time-consuming duties they plan for themselves."[94]

The Iargan notion of creativity seems to confirm this: "Creativity is thought that is continually occupied with changing the circumstances in one's life or in that of another."[95] Stefan Denaerde explains the importance that Iargans place in creativeness in terms of what they see as the purpose of their existence, which "resulted in a dominant interest in freeing themselves for individual creativity. With this idea in mind, they created a highly efficient, almost completely automated production system. Next, they sought to reduce the consumption of goods and services by appealing to the self-discipline, in order to attain a reduction in production or an increase in population. Eventually they reached the situation in which everyone, without exception, had only to work for one day in the week on the direct production process. The voluntary constraint of consumption and the equality of the non-creative work output, lead automatically to the equalization of incomes. People waive their right to consume and their needs decrease.

"Then comes the great moment in the development of the Iargan race, the control on consumption is lifted. All goods and services are freely available to all above a certain age. The individual self-discipline has come of age, material greed has been conquered. The Iargans look upon this as the beginning of the superculture. Free access to all this prosperity, for everyone, makes it impossible for an individual to be wanting when compared to others."[96]

Even when that stage is reached, the Master from Venus confirmed to Adamski, "monotony is never experienced by us. Each moment that passes is a joyous one. And it matters not what work we have to do. If what you call labor needs to be done, we do it with full joy and love in our being. And on our planet, each day brings its quota of things to be done, exactly as on yours."[97]

In one of his early messages through Benjamin Creme, World Teacher Maitreya likewise reassures us that living in harmony does not equal tedious routine, on the contrary: "Allow Me to show you the way – forward, into a simpler life where no man lacks; where no two days are alike; where the joy of Brotherhood manifests through all men."[98]

While our governments, scientists and military, since World War II, have been squandering public money, time, energy and talents to devise ever more destructive weapons, thereby allowing untold misery to continue and exacerbate for millions of people on Earth, the space people have been sharing, in their usual inconspicuous ways, crucial insights into the solutions to our problems. We may assume they did so, too, in their exchanges at government level, but the stories of many 'common' people, as compiled here, leave no doubt as to what needs to be done in a world where freedom and justice are available only to those who have the money to secure such: replace greed and competition by sharing and co-operation; abolish any kind of discrimination and establish right human relations. These, we are told, are the keys to the establishment of freedom and justice for all, which alone will guarantee lasting peace.

Sadly, the gross inequality in today's world leaves many people feeling disenfranchised, powerless and often cynical about promises of a better tomorrow. For them it is easier to dismiss the statements about a harmonious world in which freedom and justice reign for everyone as belated 'hippie' dreams, 'utopian', 'wishful thinking', et cetera. Yet, as Enrique Barrios was told: "You are approaching a decisive point in Earth evolution, a time when you either unite and bring about what some call the 'Age of Aquarius', or you destroy yourself."[99]

Wilbert Smith elaborates: "We have arrived at a time in our development when we must make a final choice between right and wrong. The people from elsewhere are much concerned about the choice which we will make, partly because it will have its repercussions on them and partly because we are their blood brothers and [they] are truly concerned with our welfare."[100]

When our systems crash, our structures crumble, and the time comes to make that crucial choice, will we choose to return to the false freedom of the 'free market', the illusion of choice that is created by wasteful squandering of resources, talents, time and energy? Or will we have the awareness and the courage to choose true freedom, that comes with freedom from fear, freedom from want, and freedom of thought?

Chapter 3 Addendum:
Iarga, Ophir and Clarion, or Mars, Venus and Saturn?

As my previous research indicates, the extraterrestrial presence on our planet originates from within our own solar system (see pages 85-86), the more elaborate argument for which can be found in Chapters 5 and 6 of *Here to Help: UFOs and the Space Brothers*. This notion finds its basis in the statements of the early contactees in the USA (Adamski, Nelson, Menger) and elsewhere (Kraspedon, Smith, Ghibaudi) and is corroborated by the information coming from the Teachers of humanity – the Ageless Wisdom teachings. The ridicule and defamation that befell these contactees provides ample reasons why others (such as Bethurum, Angelucci, Meier, Denaerde) say they were told that their contacts came from other solar systems or even galaxies. For this reason the names that they used for the home planets of their contacts have been placed in quotation marks throughout this book.

Given the urgency of the information that has been compiled in this volume, pinpointing its origin might not be the most important thing we can do with it. Yet, it might enrich and broaden our perception of the solar system if we could identify some of the planets that contactees have written about, by comparing the sometimes very detailed descriptions that have been given with the information which has been ascribed to sources from the planets in our own system.

Various contactees have shared details about their contacts which seem to be confirmed by others. Truman Bethurum, for instance, asked his contact, the captain of a saucer whom he encountered on seven or eight occasions, "if she thought that we on earth might know [their planet Clarion] by some other name, such as Mars or Jupiter... She smiled and assured me that such was not the case..."[101] Yet on a later encounter, she told him: "We have our name for things the same as the earth people have their names, and there is a possibility of having different names for the same planets or other things common to them and us..."[102] Interestingly, of Mr Bethurum's contacts, Benjamin Creme's Master has stated that they originated from Saturn.[103]

Dino Kraspedon, who – like Truman Bethurum – was invited aboard a landed saucer, relates that the captain of one of the saucers which he first saw in November 1952 said that he came from "a satellite of Jupiter"[104], while Benjamin Creme has said that the inhabitants of Jupiter "live on the various moons orbiting the planet."[105]

When Mr Kraspedon expressed his amazement at the visitor's height, he was told: "We are not all diminutive. On the same satellite we have men who are small or large, white, black or dark. Earth men are generally tall, but there are also pigmies and people of medium stature, and the white, the red, the dark, and the black. Nature reveals her unity in diversity."[106] In an editorial comment on a review of Canadian contactee Miriam Delicado's book *Blue Star*, Benjamin Creme's Master said that the tall beings in her account came from Jupiter. Creme has also given brief, but rather illuminating descriptions of some of the other planets where he says the UFOs that visit us hail from.[107]

About the people on Venus, Dino Kraspedon is told that they reach a height of six foot. "They belong to various races, predominantly a fair type. Their bodies are well made, but they are the most like Earth people, both in appearance and in spirit. They are energetic, talkative, kindly, and above all, spiritually minded."[108] The descriptions of Venusians from George Adamski and Howard Menger are very similar and corroborate Benjamin Creme's assertion that Venus is "unbelievably" advanced.

In a series of questions and answers, Dino Kraspedon's contact tells him: "On Pluto life is very similar to that on Earth. The people are identical in nearly everything. But notwithstanding their advanced intelligence, they incline to evil and neglect God. They allow their baser instincts to rule them. They learned to travel through space a long time ago. They do not war among themselves – war, alas, only exists on Earth. But they are dangerous beings, and any instances of saucers doing harm to people on Earth can be attributed to them."[109] In answer to a question about the beings on Pluto, Benjamin Creme stated that they are "[b]eings you would not like to meet on a dark night!"[110]

The Ageless Wisdom holds that every planet goes through seven rounds, or 'incarnations', each lasting millions of years. About Mars Mr Creme has said that it is at about the same stage in evolution as Earth while Venus, being in its last round, is almost perfected. However, he says, "Mars has not made as many mistakes as we have, which is why it has a technology unbelievably ahead of ours... They make most of the spacecraft we see and call UFOs, from small scout ships up to gigantic motherships. Even some of the Venusian spacecraft are made on Mars to Venusian specifications."[111] On several occasions Mr Creme has said that Mars "is the spacecraft 'factory' for our solar system; it makes about 90 per cent of all the spacecraft".[112] Benjamin Creme's Master, too, stated: "The Martians are the greatest space engineers."[113] Interestingly, Truman Bethurum was also told that "Mars is a great manufacturing planet."[114] And Adamski, too, said: "Mars, as I understand, is highly developed in science and manufacturing."[115]

When we now read Stefan Denaerde's account of what he was shown about 'Iarga', we would be forgiven for thinking that he was describing the very same planet: "They showed me two of their fully automatic factory complexes, one that produced cars and another that produced the trans-oceanic rail bridges (...) but I will spare you the details. The need to continually write in superlatives tends to bring aversion... How the Iargans can develop and build such mechanical monsters is a mystery to me. They also thought it desirable to show me the robot production of the houses... I thanked them kindly for the offer, but I had seen enough of all that automation..."[116]

Stefan Denaerde locates 'Iarga' in another solar system, "not much more than ten light years away from us."[117] He is astounded by its enormous population – which at one point he specifies at three hundred billion[118], but we can't exclude the possibility that these are some of the instances where he obliges his hosts' request to "bring in certain inexactitudes" (see page 7). Now if we see what Benjamin Creme says about the population density on Mars, again we are faced with a striking resemblance: "...there are more Martians on Mars than there are people on Earth. We have some 6.7 billion people on Earth. Mars is smaller than Earth; there are smaller people on Mars."[119]

About his hosts from 'Iarga', Stefan Denaerde wrote: "...when in action, their movements were lightning fast and emphasized their tremendous strength. They were like volcanoes. After a period of rest, they would erupt into a wave of energy and temperament that would have made a Spaniard jealous."[120] He later adds: "Their behaviour toward one another was really remarkable. I never once saw a man in the vicinity of a woman who did not put at least one arm around her. A big hug was their normal manner of greeting one another, and this also applied to the children."[121] Dino Kraspedon's says about Martians: "On Mars there are two root races: one fair and one dark. The fair race is the most tractable and gentle. The dark race is composed of people who are short of stature and of a lively disposition."[122]

According to Benjamin Creme, Mars isn't of the same evolutionary status as Venus and has three levels or zones: A, B and C. In the A zone, the top stratum, "the people are like gods, perfect beings", comparable, we may assume, to the Elder Brothers of humanity, the Masters of Wisdom. In the B zone, "there are well-evolved people but not yet perfected. On the lowest stratum, C, the people are not very evolved."[123] He has also stated that it has been three million years since life on Mars manifested on the dense physical plane of the planet, meaning that it has been on the etheric physical since then.[124]

Interestingly, in the more obscure description of the evolution of life on 'Iarga', Stefan Denaerde is told something that hints at such segregation along evolutionary lines: "Iarga, in contrast to the Earth, had a manifesting God who carried out reincarnation selection *during* the life cycle of our race. He continually picked out the selfish and therefore improved the mental polarization of the living generation. The selfish were placed in a different existence, where they followed their own development. (...) They were the last surviving group which had created indescribable suffering in the other existence..."[125] The 1982 translation adds: "On Earth, the weeds grow up with the corn until the harvest, and then the selection takes place. Because of this, mankind cannot improve her mentality. You are still troubled by the demonic element of human dualism and there is no escape. On Iarga, on the other hand, the weeds are constantly removed, which neutralizes the demonic element. (...) Due to the planet conditions, a human is wilful and disobedient. He obeys no God, no commandment, and no conscience; he even pretends that he doesn't have one. He knows everything better. (...) A large dose of unselfishness can only exist in an environment that is protected from evil."[126]

Some of the above descriptions show striking similarities between Mr Denaerde's descriptions of 'Iarga' and those of others about Mars. Although, inevitably, the information from the contactees is coloured by their own background, conditioning and disposition, it might be interesting to compare the quality or 'feel' of the communications from some of the sources.

For instance, if 'Iarga' is Mars, how do the 'colour' and the 'tone' of the communications from Adamski's contacts from Venus and Mars compare to those from Mr Denaerde's contacts? To find out, let us look at three quotations that all touch on the same topic of the innate human urge for betterment, from three different sources:

1- "Inherent in all mankind, however deeply buried it may be, is the yearning to rise to something higher. Your school system on Earth is, in a sense, patterned after the universal progress of life. For in your schools you progress from grade to grade and from school to school, toward a higher and fuller education. In the same way, man progresses from planet to planet, and from system to system toward an ever higher understanding and evolvement in universal growth and service."[127]

2- "People of Earth have become separate entities which are no longer truly human in expression as in the beginning they were. Now they are but slaves of habit. Nonetheless, imprisoned within these habits is still the original soul that yearns for expression according to its Divine inheritance. (...) And this is why, desiring finer and greater expression, more often than men realize, something stirring within the depths of their beings leaves the habit-bound self uneasy and restless."[128]

3- "The individuality expresses itself in egocentricity, greed and avarice. In the continual reaching for a material goal, a measure of satisfaction is experienced, but when the goal is reached, the satisfaction shows itself to be relative and of short duration, merely an object for comparison with what others have. So it continues toward the next goal, usually a higher income or a higher position, and the search continues, because the satisfaction lies only in the searching."[129]

The first quotation is from George Adamski's book *Inside the Space Ships* where he quotes the Master from Venus, which Benjamin Creme says is one of the most advanced planets in the solar system. The second is from the same book, but spoken by Adamski's contact Firkon from Mars, while the third quotation is from Stefan Denaerde's contacts from 'Iarga'. The first and second quotation display an equally exalted source, and while the third shows acute insight, it is markedly more prosaic. Based on Benjamin Creme's description of Mars, this seems to point to the possibility that Adamski's Martian contact was from the planet's A zone and Denaerde's from the B zone on Mars. By now, readers will not be surprised to learn that in answer to a question Benjamin Creme confirmed this latter supposition.[130]

Clearly, as with the whole subject of UFOs, no conclusive proof is possible until the time of open contact, or when we have developed etheric vision. Yet, as is shown here, interesting inferences can be made by comparing and synthesising the information from different sources. (See also Appendix I.)

Notes

1   Benjamin Creme (1979), *The Reappearance of the Christ and the Masters of Wisdom*, p.206
2   Alberto Perego (1963), *L'aviazione di altri pianeti opera tra noi: rapporto agli italiani: 1943-1963*, p.534
3   Creme (2010), *The Gathering of the Forces of Light – UFOs and their Spiritual Mission*, p.29
4   Ibidem, p.24
5   George Adamski (1955), *Inside the Space Ships*, p.165
6   Buck Nelson (1956), *My Trip to Mars, the Moon and Venus*, p.8
7   Truman Bethurum (1954), *Aboard a Flying Saucer*, p.85
8   Howard Menger (1959), *From Outer Space to You*, p.100
9   Ibid., p.163
10 Adamski (1957-58), *Cosmic Science for the Promotion of Cosmic Principles and Truth – Questions and Answers*, Series No. 1, Part No.5, Question #100
11 Adamski (1955), op cit, p.235-36
12 Ibid., p.66-67
13 Stefan Denaerde (1977), *Operation Survival Earth*, p.30
14 Adamski (1957-58), op cit, Part No.5, Question #100
15 Nelson (1956), op cit, p.5-6
16 Ibid., p.16
17 Menger (1959), op cit, p.163
18 Bethurum (1954), op cit, p.58
19 Ibid., p.72
20 Ibid., p.137
21 Nelson (1956), op cit, p.13
22 Menger (1959), op cit, p.58
23 Alice A. Bailey (1953), *A Treatise on the Seven Rays, Vol. V – Esoteric Healing*, pp.549-50
24 Denaerde (1982), *Contact from Planet Iarga*, p.91
25 Ibid., p.65
26 Adamski (1957-58), op cit, Part No.1, Question #10
27 Ibid., Question #9
28 Nelson (1956), op cit, p.11
29 Enrique Barrios (1989), *Ami, Child of the Stars*, p.12
30 Adamski (1955), op cit, p.94
31 Ibid., p.138
32 Denaerde (1977), op cit, p.59-60
33 Ibid., p.45
34 Daniel Fry (1954a), *[A Report By Alan] To Men of Earth*, in: Fry (1966), *The White Sands Incident* p.87

35 Ibid., p.91-92
36 Willy Brandt (ed.; 1980), *North-South – A Programme for Survival*, p.13
37 Benjamin Creme's Master (1989), 'The reordering of priorities', in Creme (ed.; 2004), *A Master speaks*, 3rd expanded edition, pp.145-46
38 'The Universal Declaration of Human Rights'. Available at <www.un.org/en/documents/udhr/>
39 Creme (2001), *The Great Approach – New Light and Life for Humanity*, p.20
40 Adamski (1957-58), op cit, Part No.1, Question #19
41 Adamski (1955), op cit, p.67
42 Adamski (1957-58), op cit, Part No.1, Question #18
43 Denaerde (1977), op cit, p.43
44 Desmond Leslie and George Adamski (1970), *Flying Saucers Have Landed*, Revised & Enlarged edition, p.242
45 Barrios (1989), op cit, p.76
46 Ibid., p.77
47 Ibid., pp.91-92
48 Denaerde (1977), op cit, p.41
49 Ibid.
50 Menger (1959), p.165
51 Ibid., p.163
52 Denaerde (1982), op cit, p.64
53 Denaerde (1977), op cit, p.49
54 Ibid., p.49
55 Ibid., p.58
56 Ibid., p.63
57 Ibid., p.38
58 Ibid., p.43
59 Ibid., pp.43-44
60 Ibid., p.44
61 Ibid., p.47
62 Ibid., pp.46-47
63 Ibid., p.48
64 Ibid.
65 Ibid.
66 Denaerde (1982), op cit, p.65
67 Denaerde (1977), op cit, p.47
68 Denaerde (1982), op cit, p.64
69 Denaerde (1977), op cit, p.52
70 Barrios (1989), op cit, p.90
71 Ibid., p.93
72 Ibid., p.75
73 Adamski (1955), op cit, p.241

74 Ibid., p.166
75 Adamski (1964), 'The Space People', in: Gerard Aartsen (2010), *George Adamski – A Herald for the Space Brothers*, p.113
76 Adamski (1955), op cit, p.86
77 Ibid., p.168
78 Ibid., p.184
79 Denaerde (1977), op cit, p.24
80 Ibid., p.39
81 Barrios (1989), op cit, p.92
82 Nelson (1956), op cit pp.10-11
83 Barrios (1989), op cit, p.79
84 Denaerde (1977), op cit, p.38
85 Ibid., p.32
86 Ibid., p.24
87 Ibid., p.58
88 Ibid., pp.54-55
89 Ibid., p.62
90 Ibid., p.92
91 Ibid., p.58
92 Barrios (1989), p.39
93 Adamski (1957-58), op cit, Part No.1, Question #11
94 Ibid., Part No. 2, Question #45
95 Denaerde (1977), op cit, p.61
96 Denaerde (1982), op cit, p.92
97 Adamski (1955), op cit, pp.204-05
98 Maitreya, in Creme (ed., 1980), *Messages from Maitreya the Christ*, Message No. 3, September 1977
99 Barrios (1989), op cit, p.99
100 Wilbert Smith (1969), *The Boys From Topside*, op cit, p.29

Iarga, Ophir and Clarion

101 Bethurum (1954), op cit, p.83
102 Ibid., p.103
103 Creme (ed., 2014), answers to questions, *Share International* magazine, No.6, July/August 2014, p.28
104 Dino Kraspedon (1959), *My Contact with Flying Saucers*, p.29
105 Creme (1997), *Maitreya's Mission, Vol. Three*, p.341
106 Kraspedon (1959), op cit, p.29
107 Creme (ed., 2009), editorial comment, *Share International* magazine, No.1, January/February, pp.26-27
108 Kraspedon (1959), op cit, p.190
109 Ibid., p.191
110 Creme (2001), op cit, p.135

111 Creme (2010), op cit, pp.43-44
112 Creme (2009), 'Questions and answers', *Share International* magazine, September, p.26
113 Interview with Benjamin Creme's Master. In: Creme (1997), op cit, p.194
114 Bethurum (1954), op cit, p.85
115 Adamski (1961), *Flying Saucers Farewell*, p.92
116 Denaerde (1982), op cit, pp.55-57
117 Denaerde (1977), op cit, p.27
118 Ibid., p.31
119 Creme (ed.; 2009), op cit
120 Denaerde (1977), op cit, p.24
121 Ibid., p.56
122 Kraspedon (1959), op cit, p.190
123 Creme (2010), op cit, p.44
124 Ibid., p.43
125 Denaerde (1977), op cit, p.103
126 Denaerde (1982), op cit, pp.88-89
127 Adamski (1955), op cit, pp.88-89
128 Ibid., p.116-17
129 Denaerde (1977), op cit, p.61
130 Creme (ed., 2014), op cit

Life on other planets (pp.85-86)

a Menger (1959), op cit, p.162, and Aartsen (2011), *Here to Help: UFOs and the Space Brothers*, 2nd edition 2012, p.140
b Creme (2001), *The Great Approach – New Light and Life for Humanity*, p.129
c Menger (1959), op cit, pp.126-27
d Adamski (1957-58), op cit, Part No.1, Question #12
e Adamski (1965), *Answers to Questions Most Frequently Asked About the Space Visitors and Life on Other Planets*, p.16
f Aartsen (2011), op cit, pp.92-98
g Menger (1959), op cit, p.84
h Aartsen (2011), op cit, p.92
i Steve Connor (2015), 'The galaxy collisions that shed light on unseen parallel Universe'. *The Independent*, 26 March. Available at <www.independent.co.uk/news/science/the-galaxy-collisions-that-shed-light-on-unseen-parallel-universe-10137164.html> [Accessed 27 March 2015]

4. A new civilization: We must lead the way

"The new energies of Aquarius, mounting daily in potency, are already making their presence felt, and lie behind the changes, in every sphere, which are now occurring on a global scale. These changes must, and will, reflect the quality, the inner nature, of the Aquarian energy – namely, Synthesis. These energies of Synthesis, fusing and blending the different strands of our multifaceted life, have the task of bringing humanity to an awareness of its Oneness, an appreciation of its part in the Great Plan, and an ability to manifest that Plan in right relationship on the physical plane."[1]

Thus did Benjamin Creme's Master, who has contributed an article to every issue of *Share International* magazine since its inception in January 1982, outline the threefold effect of the new energies entering the planet at the beginning of this new cosmic cycle, due to the solar system's shifting alignment from the constellation of Pisces to Aquarius. This fact is also acknowledged by several contactees, as we will see in this chapter.

Many will be aware or have heard of this impending 'new age', and even those who dismiss it as a purely mystical notion can't deny the fact of this new cosmic alignment. They might deny that distant constellations have different energetic qualities to them which affect the course of events here on Earth, but perhaps that is understandable given that humanity hasn't yet lived through the roughly 2,150-year-long cycle to manifest its effects, in the way that the current state of the planet testifies to the over-emphasis of the Piscean qualities of individuality and idealism.[2]

Yet, it would be equally difficult to deny that people are coming into their own and are no longer willing to accept authority at face value, while at the same time recognizing their strength when acting in unison. Various dramatic examples of these trends can be found in recent history, such as the people of Eastern Europe simply overrunning the oppressive border controls into Western Europe in 1989-90, the democratic transition from military rule in many South American countries, Indonesia and elsewhere, as well as the massive demand for freedom and justice as expressed in the 'Arab Spring', 'Occupy Wall Street', the 'Indignados' and similar movements, and, even as we are writing this, the tide of refugees and migrants that simply will not be stemmed by barbed wire, walls or seas. While the results of these manifestations of people power may seem temporary or even absent, the significance is in their occurrence. After all, the fall of the communist block shows that when the right time and the right people coalesce under the right impulse, even the unthinkable becomes possible.

It is for this reason that the Master from Venus told Adamski, long before the ubiquitous use of social media in today's world: "I think the people of Earth would be amazed to find how swiftly change could come throughout the planet. Now that you have the medium for world-wide broadcasting, messages urging love and tolerance for all, instead of suspicion and censure, would find receptive hearts. For the great part of the Earth's population is weary of strife and its aftermath of woe. We know that, as never before, they hunger for knowledge of a way of life that will deliver them."[3]

So where do we start? As indicated above, it starts with awareness. Barrios' Ami gives us a titillating insight into how we are asleep with our eyes wide open: "You think that life has no wonder. Therefore, you are hypnotized. You don't listen to the sea. You don't sense the aromas of the night. You take no notice of your walk or of the view. You are not aware of breathing. You are hypnotized by your own hypnosis. You think that whoever can't share your particular hypnosis is your enemy. All of this is hypnosis, all of you are hypnotized. Asleep. Each time someone begins to feel that life is beautiful, he awakens. A waking person knows that life is paradise, and he enjoys it, moment by moment. But let's not ask for so much in an uncivilized world."[4]

Therefore, the Venusian Master tells Adamski, "[y]ou must impress, as best you can, understanding in the minds of your brothers on Earth that knowledge of themselves is the first requisite. And the first questions: 'Who am I? Through what avenues can I express in order to return to the oneness from which I have fallen?' "[5] Howard Menger, too, is told the same thing: "Man must learn what he is, where he came from, and what his real purpose is here on this planet."[6]

It is this oneness with the divine principle, or Cause, from which we originate and to which we owe our existence, that the space visitors continuously refer us, as in the case of Daniel Fry's contact: "Mankind ... no matter where or when he may come into being, is endowed with the innate realization that there is an infinite intelligence and a supreme power which is greater than man's ability to comprehend. During the many stages of his development, man's attitude toward this power may vary from fear and resentment, to reverence and love. But he has always had the instinctive desire to learn more of the spiritual side of his nature and the creative sphere of this power."[7] And, "[a]s the mind of man gains in understanding and his spiritual consciousness evolves, he becomes aware of the fact that only through co-operation with man and the Spiritual Love of what he calls God can he effectively improve the conditions of his daily life."[8] For this reason, Ami says: "If you were aware of yourself, as you are of your surroundings, you would discover many things…"[9]

Note that this is not a call for a return to the simplistic religious notions that millions of people have moved on from over the past six or seven decades. Indeed, Adamski muses while on a Saturnian mothership, "So many throughout the world are unawakened to the causes behind [the problems besetting humanity]. Only when enough people realize what they are and, with their whole hearts, desire to change them by giving up their personal greeds and the desire for exaltation, one above the other, can it come to pass."[10]

Likewise, Daniel Fry's contact tells him: "Your books of philosophy state that man should love his neighbor and forgive his enemies. Our books, however, say that if a man *understands* his neighbor and his neighbor *understands* him, they will never become enemies. Understanding your fellow man requires the ability to put yourself in his place and see things as he sees them. There is a great difference between knowledge and understanding. Knowledge comes from the head but understanding comes from the heart."[11]

When we understand and know ourselves, his contact tells Mr Fry, we will recognize that "the needs and desires, the hopes and fears of all the people of your earth, are actually identical. When this fact becomes a part of everyone's understanding, then you will have a sound basis for the formation of the 'One World' of which your politicians speak so glibly and your spiritual leaders speak so wistfully."[12]

Adamski's contacts remind him once again: "We, as your brothers living on other worlds than your own, view impartially the divided groups of people on your planet. We, who have learned more regarding our Father's laws, operative throughout the Universe, cannot make the distinctions that keep you in such constant turmoil and we are saddened to see what is taking place on your Earth. We, as brothers of all mankind, are willing to help all those whom we can reach and who desire our help. But at no time may we force our way of life upon the people of your world."[13] This confirms what Daniel Fry is told: "If we were to land in both [the USA and the Soviet Union] simultaneously, the result would ... intensify the existing race for armaments. Eventually, it could bring about the very holocaust we are attempting to prevent.

"We will point out the way, and help you understand the wisdom of love and co-operation. And we will give you such help as we can[, but you and the other people whom we have contacted must spread the word and help your world to understand.] Whether or not your children will have any future to look forward to, will depend largely upon the success of your own efforts."[14] And confirming that separativeness is the cause of our ills: "[T]he possibility of atomic warfare on your earth is not the problem, it is merely a symptom and no one has ever cured an illness by treating only the symptoms."[15]

To leave no doubt lingering, Adamski pointed out to his audience: "Some people are fostering an erroneous idea that the space people are here to save a 'chosen few' in the event of nuclear warfare, or if a disaster should strike. This is totally false. Should they be in the vicinity when a catastrophe is taking place, they would do their utmost to help if possible; but they are not actually coming our way to save us from conditions into which we have placed ourselves. Each planet, each individual, must fulfill its own destiny by solving its own problems.

"The law of brotherhood has been handed down to us through countless ages. They live this law. So were they to save any peoples, it would not just be a 'chosen few'. It would be all within reach. They would not discriminate. Remember, they do not recognize our racial or religious divisions."[16]

Daniel Fry's contact Alan explained to him: "Every civilization in the Universe, no matter where or when it originates, develops primarily through the continuing increase in knowledge and *understanding* which results from the successful pursuit of 'science'." However, he elaborates, the word 'science' has a much wider scope than the reductionist approach that is so prevalent today, and he goes on to define it as "the orderly, and intelligently directed, search for truth." Alan distinguishes the three principal branches of science as (1) the physical or material science; (2) the social sciences, which describe the relationship between man and his fellow man; and (3) the spiritual science, which covers the relationship "between man and the great creative power and infinite intelligence which pervades and controls all nature".

"All of the science in the Universe, all of the search for truth and the pursuit of understanding, will come under one of these three headings or divisions. We cannot draw a sharp dividing line between them, because there are times when they will overlap, but the fundamental laws which govern all three divisions are identical. If any civilization in the Universe is to develop fully and successfully, each of the three branches of science must be pursued with equal effort and diligence." In contrast with our present emphasis on the material science, Alan says, "[t]he Spiritual and Social sciences, however, must come first. There can be no dependable development of a material science until you have first built a firm foundation of spiritual and social science."[17]

That social science – of properly relating to our fellow human beings – is not confined or limited to academics, but should be put into practice, is a common theme running through the accounts of all the original contactees. For instance, George Adamski told his listeners: "I can assure you of one thing, the space people are not coming merely to satisfy our personal curiosity. At the present time, I have been told, the best way we can help is by beginning to live with more respect toward one another. For as this is done throughout the world, fear and hostility between the peoples will diminish; leaving a fertile field in which to work for the betterment of all. But final success in this depends upon each individual. (...)

"We must learn to live humbly, respecting our fellow man regardless of his color of skin or position in life. But this is a problem each person, and each nation, must solve individually."[18] In other words, real change can only come from within, and only if we manifest it – there's arguably no point in attaining awareness of right human relations or anything else, and not giving it expression in the way we relate to others.

The effect of such a change cannot be fathomed for, he adds, "each individual is a radiating center of influence, whose ultimate circumference no one can accurately perceive. Watch your thoughts and see if they are of the type you really desire to entertain. If not, change them to conform with your better aspirations. Become the master of your mind ... not its slave. Watch your attitude toward others – business contacts, friends, strangers, members of your own family. Are you polite to some, tolerant toward others, and argumentative with those closest to you? Or are you compassionate and kind to all alike? The world as a whole is composed of billions of individuals, each of whom

Huge fleet of 1,500 UFOs sighted over Guadalajara, Mexico on 23 October 2011 (above) and a fleet of unknown size over Sacramento, California, USA on 13 August 2011 (below).

is important as a radiating center of action. And the whole cannot be changed unless, and until, each small part is brought into cooperation and harmonious coordination with all others. In the human family, we know this as the Brotherhood of Man."[19]

Like the expectation of further revelation by a new or returned Teacher (see pages 43-44) and the commandment to treat others as we would like to be treated (Appendix II), the notion of a shift or expansion of consciousness is also shared by all major religions, recognizing it as essential to personal development. The book *Presence – Human Purpose and the Field of the Future* gives an interesting and concise summary of how the idea of shifting consciousness is expressed in the various traditions. In the esoteric Christian tradition it is associated with 'grace' or 'revelation'; Taoism speaks of the transformation of vital energy (qing) into subtle life force (qi) and spiritual energy (shi); Buddhists strive after 'cessation' of thought, or 'enlightenment'; in Hinduism it is referred to as 'wholeness' and in mystical Islam it is known as 'opening the heart'.[20] The Venusian Master put it thus: "The purpose of life on other worlds is basically the same as yours. Inherent in all mankind, however deeply buried it may be, is the yearning to rise to something higher. Your school system on Earth is, in a sense, patterned after the universal progress of life. For in your schools you progress from grade to grade and from school to school, toward a higher and fuller education. In the same way, man progresses from planet to planet, and from system to system toward an ever higher understanding and evolvement in universal growth and service."[21]

Yet again, we find reason to heed the Teachers, rather than dismiss their teachings for the limited interpretations of organised religions that have grown around these.

With the collapse of the world economy mankind will come to

its senses and, Benjamin Creme's Master has said, "men will come to realize their oneness. (...) Sharing, justice and freedom will grow in men's minds as powerful symbols of the future, as inherent rights of all, the way to correct relationship."[22]

Indeed, one of the first practices we will need to implement when we want to give expression to our restored sense of oneness and our consciousness expanded to include our fellow man, will be the adequate redistribution of the available food, natural resources, technological know-how, energy, et cetera, to supply every man, woman and child on the planet with the basic necessities for life. However, this will not mean paradise – real or imagined – overnight, as the Tibetan Master DK indicates: "[T]he 'principle of sharing' will be a recognised motivating concept of the new civilisation. This will not involve beautiful, sweet and humanitarian attitudes. The world will still be full of selfish and self-seeking people, but public opinion will be such that certain fundamental ideals will motivate business, being forced upon business by public opinion; the fact that the new general ideas will in many cases be governed by the expediency of interplay will not basically matter. It is the sharing that is of importance."[23]

Even though humanity or the world as a whole have yet to embrace the principle of sharing as the key to create the trust that is necessary to rid the world of injustice, there is an unseen and largely unreported, yet growing movement in implementing it on a smaller scale.

One striking example is the Transition Towns movement in which communities share responsibility for reducing their carbon footprint and reduce waste to fight resource depletion. In an article about the movement Rob Hopkins, one of the founders, says: "People know major changes have to be made in the face of climate change and resource depletion. It started with friends and neighbours saying 'what can we do as ordinary people knowing that our governments are not going to sort it out'." In Portugal, environmental journalist Stephen Leahy writes, "where unemployment is over 20 per cent and wages are depressed, the Transition Movement is focused on reducing the need to use money. One small town banned money for three days. People shared or exchanged services instead. (...) There are now [2013] over 1,000 communities involved in Transition Towns, a volunteer, non-profit movement. These communities are inventing their own ways to reduce their dependence on fossil fuels while increasing local resilience and self-sufficiency in food, water, energy, culture and wellness." Among several other people, Mr Leahy quotes Celine Bilsson, a member of the renewable energy commission of the French rural village of Saint-Gilles-Du-Mene in Brittany which now produces 30 per cent of its own energy through renewable sources: "We didn't spend time doing studies. We just reacted. You just do it."[24] Since its inception, the Transition Towns movement has grown into a worldwide Transition Network with an annual international conference where participants "connect, create, share and celebrate".[25]

As for implementing the principle of sharing towards food security for everyone, anti-hunger and social rights activist José Luis Vivero Pol describes inspiring examples of people joining forces in an organized way to produce, exchange and consume food outside the prevalent market logic, "like community-supported agriculture in the US, joint purchasing groups in Spain and France or urban gardens with free food access in Belgium. Everywhere you see these short and local chains of consumers and producers who organize themselves to produce and consume better food." He adds that "none of these arrangements are new to human societies. For thousands of years human beings have been organizing traditional collective activity to produce food. All over the world, especially in Africa and Asia, you can find collective property of natural resources and land plots that are managed in a collective way. That's why I say that these ideas about the transformation of the food system [from a commodity to a commons] aren't just a theoretical or naïve wishful thinking. Collective action for food is already ongoing in developed and developing countries."[26]

Writing about a recent development in South America in *Share International* magazine, Thiago Staibano Alves describes the rise of the 'business without bosses' movement. He says that while "many theories of modern business management and human resources speak of the importance of workers in companies and factories, in fact, limited participation is allowed employees in the formulation of policies with regard to production, wages and sales policies". However, he says, a new business model has been emerging in recent decades: "Though they are still relatively few in number their growth denotes a new consciousness emerging in the world of work – more egalitarian, more participatory and socially responsible. It also shows that such experiments are bringing gains to workers and their communities." He then goes on to describe a number of examples in Brazil, Argentina and Venezuela of such 'businesses without bosses', where "workers define policies for production, wages and sales usually through worker assemblies". In Latin America and some other countries, Alves writes, "worker-ownership has developed into a powerful way for people to defend their rights against steadily growing labor deregulation".[27]

The idea of co-operatives is, of course, nothing new. Many are typically small to medium-sized businesses, although there is an example of a large co-operative business that is as well-known as it is successful. Founded in London in the early

1920s, the John Lewis Partnership now has 90,000 partners who own 44 shops and 300 supermarkets, an online and catalogue business, a production unit and a farm, and all share in the benefits and profits. The Partnership has its own constitution which states that the happiness of its members is the Partnership's ultimate purpose, recognising that such happiness depends on having a satisfying job in a successful employee-owned business. The constitution also establishes a system of "rights and responsibilities" and defines mechanisms to provide for the Partnership's management, "with checks and balances to ensure accountability, transparency and honesty".[28] While the pay ratio at John Lewis between the highest and the lowest paid jobs of 75:1 is still a long way off from the equality on 'Iarga', as described in the previous chapter, it is less skewed than the obscene 422:1, 323:1 and similar CEO-to-worker pay ratios[29] that are symptomatic of the current cut-throat capitalist system.

The manifestation of this new awareness is also observed by journalist and writer Paul Mason, who writes: "[W]e're seeing the spontaneous rise of collaborative production: goods, services and organisations are appearing that no longer respond to the dictates of the market and the managerial hierarchy. (...)

"Almost unnoticed, in the niches and hollows of the market system, whole swaths of economic life are beginning to move to a different rhythm. Parallel currencies, time banks, cooperatives and self-managed spaces have proliferated, barely noticed by the economics profession, and often as a direct result of the shattering of the old structures in the post-2008 crisis."

"You only find this new economy if you look hard for it. In Greece, when a grassroots NGO mapped the country's food co-ops, alternative producers, parallel currencies and local exchange systems they found more than 70 substantive projects and hundreds of smaller initiatives ranging from squats to carpools to free kindergartens. To mainstream economics such things seem barely to qualify as economic activity – but that's the point. They exist because they trade, however haltingly and inefficiently, in the currency of post-capitalism: free time, networked activity and free stuff. It seems a meagre and unofficial and even dangerous thing from which to craft an entire alternative to a global system, but so did money and credit in the age of Edward III."[30]

Most jobs nowadays do not require or allow for much creativity, if any. Yet, according to Stefan Denaerde's contacts, "[i]t is creativity that drives men to do 'even more' or 'even better.' There are two kinds of creativity, the material and the immaterial. The first is the individual striving to improve his own living standards. This is done mostly in the field of sex, property and power and is the cause of all the misery on this planet. The individuality expresses itself in egocentricity, greed and avarice. In the continual reaching for a material goal, a measure of satisfaction is experienced, but when the goal is reached, the satisfaction shows itself to be relative and of short duration, merely an object for comparison with what others have. So it continues toward the next goal, usually a higher income or a higher position, and the search continues, because the satisfaction lies only in the searching."

Immaterial creativity, on the other hand, "is lasting happiness. It is the continual striving to improve the living standards of others. It expresses itself in helpfulness, understanding, pity, tolerance, friendliness, esteem – in short, the total concept of unselfish love."[31]

It is interesting in this respect to read the pleas for a total revision of our current educational system from one of Stefan

Denaerde's fellow industrialists and fellow Dutchman. In a keynote talk in 2011, Tex Gunning, member of the executive board of Dutch multinational AkzoNobel advocated that education should not be knowledge-based, but value-based. He said that education should teach children to know themselves and live with self-confidence; to love learning and discovering; to be equipped for a stable social life; to live in coexistence with fellow human beings and with nature; and from there be capable of a valuable contribution to society.[32]

In answer to a question about how a business might be run in the spirit of sharing, Benjamin Creme suggested that instead of employing people that you will pay as little as possible for the longest hours possible, "[y]ou might start your new business as a co-operative. You employ 20 people, for example, and share the money you make. No one gets more than the others. Everyone works as hard as everyone else. You try to keep the hours you all work to a minimum and pay everyone the maximum for what they do. It is the New Age formula. When you begin to work in this way you understand what is meant by synthesis; that way you create groups. The energy of Aquarius only works in a synthetic way – through groups. It has no individual application. You have to transform your whole idea of making money and becoming rich. If you do it the Aquarian way you're not going to become fantastically rich or you are *all* going to become rich."[33]

That said, sharing in the sense of creating justice as the prerequisite for world peace and freedom for all, according to Mr Creme, "means sharing the world's resources – it is not an individual matter, but can only take place on a global scale."[34]

According to Enrique Barrios, the Age of Aquarius is "a new evolutionary stage of the planet Earth, the end of millennia of barbarism, a New Age of love, a kind of 'maturation.' You have already entered the 'Age of Aquarius,' but only in time, not in deed. The Earth begins to be ruled by other kinds of laws and cosmic geological radiations. To put it another way, there is more love in people, but they still continue to follow principles that have belonged to earlier, inferior levels of evolution. What occurs is a clash between what people feel internally and what they are obliged to do externally."[35]

With stress and frustration building fast in humanity as a result, Benjamin Creme cautions against a radical overhaul that overzealous activists would prefer: "We will not get rid of capitalism. We will give it a place in our society. It is not necessary to think in extremes, in black and white. No one ever thinks of these working together but Maitreya puts it this way: think of a cart. If you only have one wheel – whether capitalism or socialism – it will not go. All economic structures of the future will retain the balance of socialism and capitalism. Today there is no country in the world that has the balance right. From the Masters' point of view, the best balance is 30 per cent capitalism and 70 per cent socialism."[36]

Reminiscent of what Stefan Denaerde was shown about the economy on 'Iarga', even in the 1940s the Master DK predicted of the new economic system: "Private enterprise will still exist, but will be regulated; the great public utilities, the major material resources and the sources of planetary wealth – iron, steel, oil and wheat, for instance – will be owned in the first place by a governing, controlling international group; they will, however, be prepared for international consumption by national groups chosen by the people and under international direction."[37]

On many occasions Benjamin Creme has said there already exist "blueprints which if implemented would solve the redistribution problems at the heart of our economic problem today. The resources are there. There is more food in the world than we need, much of it rotting away in the storehouses of the developed world while millions die of hunger elsewhere. (...) First of all, each nation would be asked to make known what they make, what they grow, what they import. In this way the total goods of the Earth would be known. Each nation would be asked to donate to a central pool that which it has in excess of its needs. (...) Out of that central pool, created by all the nations, the needs of all would be met. This is taking into account the needs of the planet."[38]

At the same time, he says, "We are not all at the same level. We do not all believe in the same things, we do not all want the same things for humanity. Some people have a sense of the oneness of humanity which is absent from others. So everything takes time and energy, the new energies of Aquarius to bring us to a point of change. This is beginning to happen now and humanity is awakening to this promise."[39]

Mr Creme's Master said it thus: "Not revolution but evolution is [World Teacher] Maitreya's advocacy. He knows well that revolution precipitates conflict and carnage, replacing one set of problems by another. What is required is a step by step process of change which allows everyone the experience of being involved in their own destiny. Sharing is the sole means of ensuring such a process; sharing alone will engender the trust essential even to begin."[40]

Many people, both in the field of Ufology and outside, have dismissed the hopeful messages of the early contactees by simplifying them to the point of distortion. They would have us believe that these are Messianic messages that promise salvation so people will no longer need to think or act for themselves. First-hand reading of the books and pamphlets that these pioneer contactees have written to inform the world of their experiences shows quite the opposite, as one after the other exhorts humanity to take responsibility to right the wrongs in our world.

It is no coincidence that in every such case of contact, the space people emphasise the free will of mankind to determine our own future. And the fact that the Space Brothers are here to assist in building the platform for humanity's and the planet's transition into a new civilization – as the first manifestation in the next stage of our evolution – does not mean they are willing to trespass our free will. When someone asked him if he advocates the form of government used on other planets for the nations on Earth George Adamski said: "I advocate nothing! Before any change can be successful, the people must first thoughtfully consider it; then establish a sincere desire by attuning their minds beforehand. (...)

"Their form of government has been explained to us merely as an illustration to prove that the Laws for Living, as given to us countless times through the ages, are applicable on any planet. Earthlings, because of their deep reverence for these great Teachers, have enshrined their teachings in the world religions, not comprehending they were showing us a way of life. (...) Once more we are being reminded of this pattern for living. Each man, woman, and child must seek deep within himself for his own answer. For, as in all things, the whole is only as strong as its weakest link."[41]

Adamski's Martian contact Firkon adds elsewhere: "[S]o long as men do not desire to change their way of living, none can help them. Those few on Earth who do sincerely desire to learn the laws of the Infinite One must try to lead the others. And we of other worlds will help them."[42] Yet, he says, "Each individual lives his own life, makes his own future destiny, and writes his own history. In the Cosmic Plan no man is ever left stranded without hope. Once the desire is awakened in a man's heart for a better understanding of himself, his purpose for being and his relationship to the Cosmic All, the way is always opened for him to attain his goal."[43]

On his last reported sojourn on a Venusian mothership George Adamski's hosts acknowledged "that you are approaching the Cosmic Age, however little you may understand this".[44] Yet, as the developments documented earlier in this chapter show, a new spirit can be detected among mankind, which Benjamin Creme and others have been talking about in terms of the energies of Aquarius, and of which the increasing willingness of the masses to stand up for justice and freedom seems to testify.

It is only to be expected that such new energies lead to a crisis of consciousness, which currently manifests itself in the economic field. George Adamski noted: "When studying [the Bible for evidence of visitors from space], it is well to note that almost every recorded visitation from 'heaven' occurred when Earthlings found themselves in great difficulty. Then as now, the masses were not contacted, but individuals were selected here and there. The visitors gave counsel in olden times which, when followed, revived an imperilled civilization; but when ignored, that civilization eventually sank into oblivion. Today, we again stand at a momentous crossroads. The space travelers are doing their utmost to warn and help us. But the final decision lies in our hands."[45]

In the wake of the 'Occupy' protests a referendum in Switzerland was held on limiting the salaries and bonuses of company executives to a maximum of 15 times the average salary of their employees. As if predicting the outcome of the referendum, journalist Roberto Savio wrote: "[A]s the Swiss referendum shows, it is not awareness that is lacking: it is political will."[46]

Obviously, for substantial change to be effected, this means a sufficiently large section of humanity will have to take action on its own behalf, and Stefan Denaerde's contacts pointed out the major problem in this respect: "The biggest problem in the coming selection is the lukewarm, lazy, average man. These are people with roughly a nil polarization. They are not egoistic and not altruistic; they are neither flesh nor fish. For these people a great stress situation must be created, in which they must choose, whether they want to or not. (...) If you read Matthew 24 and Mark 13, you will see that Christ prophesied polarization within humanity..."[47]

According to Benjamin Creme, it is the energy of Love which the World Teacher brings that is currently saturating the planet and stimulating the good and the bad so that "humanity will see very clearly what it has to do. If this did not happen, we might feel that we might soldier on as we are. (...) The Sword of Cleavage sharpens the differences and makes clear the options before humanity. (...) We take the right way of right human relationship, of construction and harmony, on the one hand, or the way of wrong human relations and eventually total destruction for everyone, on the other."[48]

On the momentous day when the World Teacher will declare his true status to the world around the time of the final collapse of our current structures, he will also give humanity a profound experience of their oneness, of which Mr Creme's Master says: "[M]en will know afresh the joy of full participation in the realities of Life, will feel connected one to another, like the memory of a distant past". This, he says, will inspire men to "engage themselves in the work of reconstruction, the rehabilitation of the world."[49]

Returning to the notion that lasting change can only come as the result of an inner awareness, Stefan Denaerde's hosts explain: "Mental polarization is the changing of the direction of the power to love inwards – egoism – or outwards – altruism. This is not bounded by the law of action and reaction; it is a process that lies within each individual."[50] And even in 1954 Daniel Fry was reassured: "Your race and your culture, however, are not doomed to extinction. They may continue upon their upward course until they have left this danger behind them forever. The choice, you see, is yours."[51]

Once we have made that choice on a worldwide scale there is no end to what is possible when we realize we are One and act from that realization, as Truman Bethurum's contacts reassure us: "We have not the problems that you have, because we know what is right and want to do it. The same could be true upon your earth. God has been liberal with his blessings, and there is no dearth. Your peoples could amalgamate and act in unison instead of constantly warring upon each other, and then you'd find your earth worth living upon. Your deserts and plains could be transformed into gardens that would be like heaven. The substance and effort and life spent each year on your wars would bring an abundance of water into your deserts, if not from your polluted rivers from the atmosphere itself, or from your distant oceans. These things can be done. And you'd have a very paradise in which to build your homes and rear your children and see your sons bloom into manhood in peace, without the nagging horror and fear of bloody death and maimed and crazed young bodies…"[52]

In this respect, George Adamski reminds us: "[A]ll planets
#149 are school rooms in the Cosmos. And just as we graduate from grade to grade in our school systems, retaining and using knowledge learned in the lower grades, so we graduate from planet to planet and system to system. The Cosmos is a vast school with many departments of learning for every state of being. There are primary planets, and planets advanced far beyond the scope of

our earthly imaginations. But we are eligible, eventually, for all. What we need to concern ourselves with here, is to try to master the lessons of the present that we may the more speedily inherit the future that is surely our destiny."[53]

In recent years, disclosure advocates have organized petitions and a citizens' hearing to push for disclosure of what governments know about the extraterrestrial presence. While such activities are useful to keep the extraterrestrial presence in the public eye, these will clearly not save the planet. We know the space visitors are here, even as our governments deny it. We know there are cleaner and safer sources of energy that have been bought up and shelved by the fossil fuel industry. What matters is that we now know where real change starts and how to achieve or command it, by giving expression to the knowledge that has been lingering in our innermost being. As Daniel Fry's contact Alan tells him: "Your greatest era, your Golden Age, lies just before you. You have only to go through the proper door. When you increase your understanding, you will speed up the time when that Golden Age will be reached."[54]

It seems Wilbert Smith was told the same thing: "In time, when certain events have transpired, and we are so oriented that we can accept these people from elsewhere, they will meet us freely on the common ground of mutual understanding and trust, and we will be able to learn from them and bring about the Golden Age all men everywhere desire deep within their hearts."[55]

Confirming the statements of many of his fellow contactees in the previous chapter, he concludes: "We have been told of a way of life which is utopian beyond our dreams, and the means of attaining it. Can it be that such a self-consistent, magnificent philosophy is the figment of the imaginations of a number of misguided morons? I do not think so. If the only evidence we

Planets as school rooms in the Cosmos

Is there any evidence that people from one planet incarnate on another? Of course there are cases of individuals who make such claims for themselves, and anything they say by way of offering proof or evidence can only be accepted in good faith, or not. There are, however, some cases for which independent evidence or outside corroboration is available.

In my book *George Adamski – A Herald for the Space Brothers* I quote several sources that indicate George Adamski was in fact a soul from Venusian humanity who had incarnated on Earth to fulfil the mission that he became famous for.

For instance, in *The Scoriton Mystery – Did Adamski Return?* Ernest Arthur Bryant describes how on 24 April 1965, one day after Adamski died, he met three beings from a flying saucer that had landed in Dartmoor, UK one of whom identifies himself saying "My name is Yamski," or something that sounded like that, who had a tendency towards an American accent, but said "We are from Venus." He also said, "If only Des Les were here, he would understand," in a clear reference to Desmond Leslie.[a]

Similarly, in 1980, during an encounter with his contacts from space, Italian contactee Giorgio Dibitonto is introduced to another man "who impressed us immediately with his kindliness and amiability. He smiled like one who had much to say, but would not speak. 'His name is George,' said Raphael, nodding in my direction, 'the same as yours. This, our brother, lived for a while on Earth, where he chose to come on an assignment. Now he has returned to us.' "[b] When Wendelle Stevens, who published Dibitonto's story in the US, asked Benjamin Creme if Dibitonto's contacts were indeed from Venus, Mr Creme replied that it was true, adding that there were many Venusians among us then, and even today.[c]

In his 1958 novel *The Amazing Mr Lutterworth*, about which he said it was based on Adamski's mission and 75 per cent non-fiction, Desmond Leslie clearly hints that his one-time co-author had come from another planet, and did not remember it until much later in life. According to the

George Adamski Foundation, Adamski himself had warned against any claims that he would return, or had returned. However, as a warning against imposters who might try to hijack or capitalize on his legacy after his death, the above-mentioned episodes do not necessarily contradict Adamski's statement.

In another case, the Russian *Pravda* newspaper published a report by Gennady Belimov on 10 March 2004 based on a story from members of an expedition to an anomalous zone north of the Volgograd region in Russia, referred to by most people as the Medvedetskaya Ridge. One night, when the expedition members were sitting around the campfire, 7-year-old Boris Kipriyanovich asked everyone's attention: " 'Turned out, he wanted to tell them all about life on Mars, about its inhabitants and their flights to earth,' shares one of the witnesses. Silence followed. It was incredible! The little boy with gigantic lively eyes was about to tell a magnificent story about the Martian civilization (...), life of which he knew in details since he happened to descend there from Mars, had friends there." According to the report, many of those present were stunned not only by the boy's profound knowledge and intellect, but also by his eloquence.

Boriska, as he was known then, was born on 11 January 1996 in Volzhskiy. His father was a retired officer and his mother a dermatologist who told the reporter that even at two years old Boriska would "sit in a lotus position and start all these talks. He would talk about Mars, about planetary systems, distant civilizations. We couldn't believe our own ears. How can a kid know all this? Cosmos, never-ending stories of other worlds and the immense skies, are like daily mantras for him since he was 2."[d]

In an editorial comment to a report about this story in *Share International* magazine Benjamin Creme's Master confirmed the boy's origin, though adding that some of his information was not accurate.[e]

Interestingly, over the years Benjamin Creme has indicated for several well-known historical figures that they had in fact incarnated on Earth from other planets, such as William Shakespeare (from Jupiter), Maria Callas (from Mars), and Leonardo da Vinci (from Mercury).[f]

Notes on page 162

had was philosophical, we might justifiably suspect it, but when coupled with the reality of observations, thousands of them, we cannot dismiss it so easily."[56] The Venusian Master confirmed this, when he said: "[N]o man lives who has never once dreamed of what you call Utopia, or the nearly perfect world. There is nothing which man has never imagined which is not, somewhere, a reality. And, therefore, nothing that is not possible of achievement. For you too, on Earth, this is possible. For us on the other planets of our galaxy, it is so now."[57]

A glimpse of the magnificent world that is possible was given by Benjamin Creme's Master: "Imagine then a future where no man lacks for aught. Where the talents and creativity of all men demonstrate their divine origin. Where war has no place in their thoughts and where goodwill casts its benevolent net over the hearts and minds of all.

"Imagine cities of light lit by Light Itself; nowhere to be found the squalor and deprivation of today; imagine transport, fast and silent, powered by light alone, the far-off worlds and even the stars brought within our reach. Such a future awaits the men and women who have the courage to share. Such a future awaits those brave ones who love Freedom. Such a glorious future awaits those who long to understand the meaning and purpose of life."[58]

With governments covering up the extraterrestrial presence, his contacts Ilmuth and Kalna told Adamski in the 1950s that disclosure would require pressure from the masses, already stressing the importance of people power. Sixty-odd years on, with official disclosure amounting, in the words of Benjamin Creme, to nothing less than political suicide for the ruling class[59], their observation seems to apply even more to the need for change, which itself will lead to disclosure by force of Earth's

On 15 February 2012, between 7 and 8:15 am, Mr Bernd Nachreicher saw a light phenomenon on the webcam at Vilshofen Airport, some 170km north-east of Munich, Germany, which he thought resembled a Christ-like figure. When asked about it, the lens manufacturer explained it as a light refraction in the lens. (Source: TZ.de)

According to Benjamin Creme's Master the shape, representing a rocket, was manifested by the World Teacher and is a symbol for a future technology that will take mankind to the furthest reaches of the solar system and beyond. (*Share International* magazine, April 2012, p.12) re-integration into the cosmic community: "[I]t would seem that the answer lies largely with the ordinary man in the street, multiplied by his millions the world over." To which Firkon adds: "They would be your strength and if they would speak out against war in sufficient numbers everywhere, some leaders in different parts of your world would listen gladly."[60]

Enrique Barrios' protagonist Ami pointed out that informing humanity is a process, rather than a one-time spectacle, and reiterated the need for such increased awareness to be expressed by mankind if it is to do us any good: "We fulfilled our obligation by offering our help, by serving. Humanity must now make an effort on its own behalf."[61]

While clarifying the notion that we must take responsibility for our world and our future, Firkon, through Adamski, at the same time denounced the resignation or complacency that is implied in deferring our problems to 'an act of God' or a case of 'bad karma': "We recognize man as the highest representation of Deity, the consummation of all lesser forms. Should we with hurtful intent harm any form, we know that we would be forcing that form to turn from its natural purpose and do us harm. You can see why the Creator has left us all to work out our own problems. When His laws are disobeyed, they witness against us. (…) [O]nly by opposing the Divine principle can one create the inharmonious conditions which you have credited to satan, and which you yourselves must correct. (...) For all distortion must be corrected by the one who distorts."[62]

Daniel Fry's contact confirms this in no uncertain terms: "If we were to appear as members of a superior race, coming from above to lead the people of your world, we would seriously disrupt the ego balance of your civilization. Tens of millions of people, in their desperate need to avoid being demoted to second place in the universe, would go to any conceivable lengths to disprove or deny our existence. If we took steps to force the realization of our reality upon their consciousness, then about thirty per cent of these people would insist on considering us as Gods, and would attempt to place upon us all responsibility for their own welfare. Of the remaining seventy per cent, most would consider that we were potential tyrants who were planning to enslave their world, and many would immediately begin to seek means to destroy us."[63]

It is easy to see, therefore, that any attempts to denounce the experiences of the pre-disinformation contactees as escapism are in fact malicious fabrications, apparently with the aim to discredit their information. We live in a time, though, that will soon show their messages are now more urgent and relevant than ever, and indeed pertinent to humanity's salvation of itself and the planet.

More people than ever sense that change is in the air. Tapping into the massive thoughtform that has built up around this momentous time in human history, many claim prophetic qualities for their colourful daydreams of 'global ascension', 'opening stargates', 'galactic activation', and similar ways of describing the awakening of humanity to its oneness. Hence it is good to remind ourselves that the solution isn't simply awareness, but how we give it expression in practical terms.

Elsewhere I quoted George Adamski's affirmation that "[k]nowledge is useless unless it is combined with action".[64] In the same spirit Daniel Fry's contact summarizes exactly what it takes to build a new world that will ensure the survival of the race and the safe progress of its civilization, as well as the end of our cosmic isolation: "If any great and lasting good is to come from our efforts, the actual leaders must be your own people..."[65]

Chapter 4 Addendum:
The message and the source

When Adamski was picked up by his contacts Firkon and Ramu for a farewell meeting on board a Venusian mothership in August 1954, they addressed his sadness by reassuring him: "[Y]ou are losing us only in bodily form. Don't forget we can still communicate mentally, wherever we are."[66] Nevertheless, he himself cautioned against the messages from mystical channels, saying: "...I know of no psychic or mystic who understands what he or she is dealing with. And under these circumstances they are open to all types of impressions from impersonators and false prophets."[67]

One often heard objection to the information which the contactees received from their contacts is that it was "evangelical". Perhaps, in a way this is understandable given that the world was fast secularising and a generally 'materialistic' view of life took precedence, as we had long lost sight of the underlying spiritual realities such as have been reiterated in much of the current volume.

While several of the early contactees seemed to be mystically inclined, it is good to remember they were contacted by more highly evolved people than themselves (and most of us), and they tried to encapsulate their experience and the information they received in exalted language. George Adamski, moreover, received much of his information from two Masters of Wisdom, one from Venus and one from Saturn, even though he later expressed regrets about using the term 'Master' and went so far as to claim there "are no spiritual Masters anywhere"[68] (although he studied with them in Tibet as a teenager[69]) because so many people are prone to attribute – and transfer – authority and responsibility to others. However, Masters are only called so because they have 'mastered' their lower nature, and thereby the laws of nature, by learning to live according to the Laws of Life, and so have learned to express their innate divinity in physical manifestation to relative perfection – a process that every human being is involved in before he can enter the spiritual kingdom of nature (see also pages 43-44).

Despite the multitude of claims in 'new age' circles of people 'channelling' messages from one or several alleged 'Masters', the real Elder Brothers of mankind communicate only through mental telepathy, as do the Space Brothers. Benjamin Creme describes channelling thus: "In its modern, general connotation it describes the reception of teaching, information, or instruction from the astral planes (...) through an astral sensitive or medium. The information and teaching thus received, it should be understood, will suffer from the distorting mechanism of the astral planes – the planes of illusion."[70] Elsewhere he says: "[A] great deal of money is made by the channels for private 'guidance' or from the vast sale of books, while some of the teachings are generally 'uplifting' for the aspirational type. Above all, I suppose, a great many channels are confused as to the nature of their sources or 'guidance' and feel that they are performing some beneficial work of service."[71]

Adamski explained the nature of the astral planes as follows: "Two and ½ billion people [the world population at that time] are broadcasting thoughts of expectation as to what they think will occur. Most prophecies are nothing more than the influence of these thoughts. People with little understanding of the human mind receive these thoughts and believe they are messages from space people or a revelation from God. Because a small percentage of these thoughts must of necessity be correct, people become ensnared and believe they are in contact with actual entities..."[72]

Adamski told his audiences repeatedly that "there is a decided difference between telepathic communications of a universal nature, and the psychic 'messages' so commonly received and known to Earth. Until Earth's people become better acquainted with themselves and the operation of their mind, it will be difficult for them to differentiate between information received from a universal source, and that received from the thought forms encompassing our planet. For centuries of human habitation and thinking, along with the emanations from Nature herself, have resulted in vibrations far more real than most people realize. So, extreme care must be exercised not to confuse these thought forms and emanations with true telepathic communications."[73]

Firkon told Adamski in this respect: "Apart from our physical missions on Earth, all of us must hold firmly to the belief that the peoples of Earth will themselves awaken to the disaster toward which they are moving." Ramu added: "We know that the power of this thought continually sent out to all our Earth brothers has changed the hearts of many."[74]

We find this notion corroborated in Enrique Barrios' book, whose protagonist Ami says: "...we shall send 'messages' on mental frequencies. These 'messages', in the air, like radio waves, reach all people. Some of you can tune in, others cannot."[75] And: "On evolved worlds there are persons who receive and transmit them. (...) In the non-evolved worlds (...) the receivers are 'prophets' of greater or lesser degree, depending on the purity with which they transmit their reception to their world."[76] Ami also says: "Some people distort our messages through their own ideas or beliefs, but there are those who express them quite purely."[77]

However, telepathic communication, Orthon told Adamski, is a *"unified state of consciousness* between two points, the sender and the receiver, and it is the method of communication most commonly used on our planets, especially on planet Venus. Messages can be conveyed between individuals on our planet, from our planet to our space craft wherever they may be, and from planet to planet. As I said before – and let me make this firm in your memory – space or 'distance,' as you call it, is no barrier whatsoever. (...) [O]ne thing we want you to make clear to all is that the mental contacts we have been discussing are definitely *not* what your people call 'psychic' or 'spiritualistic,' but direct messages from one mind to another."[78]

Howard Menger said that when one meets the space people "one knows innately that one's every thought is bared under powerful telepathic observation. And with such knowledge one suddenly realizes he cannot hide anything, and becomes completely honest, both with himself and the visitors. It is a refreshing, cleansing feeling, which carries over into everyday dealings with one's fellow men."[79]

While telepathy has thus far been the method most commonly employed by the Masters of Wisdom to convey their teachings through their disciples in the everyday world – notably Madame Blavatsky, Alice A. Bailey and Benjamin Creme – there is also a higher form, called 'overshadowing' which Benjamin Creme says, "in the spiritual sense, is the method by which a greater conscious-ness works through one of a somewhat less developed level, thus bringing down his consciousness to humanity."[80] According to the Ageless Wisdom teaching, this is how, for instance, the Christ worked through his then-disciple Jesus from the time of the bap-tism in the river Jordan until the crucifixion[81] and how the Buddha worked through the Prince Gautama, from the time when the prince reached 'enlightenment' underneath the Bodhi tree.[82]

When asked about some of the channelled messages from alleged 'space people', Adamski said that "upon reading them carefully I have found bits of truth scattered here and there. But this is always the case; for falseness could not exist if it were not for the real from which it is patterned. It is the presence of these little points of truth that causes so much confusion in the minds of those who sincerely seek reality, but who want it on a factual rather than a mystical basis. If anything is universal, it will blend but not divide. While I do not deny the existence of people on planets beyond our system who are both higher and very much lower than ourselves in development, why should we follow 'guidance' from anyone who cannot help us? With our present distrustful attitude toward one another, surely we do not need to reach out into space to add to our divisions."[83]

He also cautioned when "names and identifications, such as position and rank, are used by the giver of the messages. As stated in *Inside the Space Ships*, space people use neither position nor name to identify them. These are personality. Nor do they ever prophecy our future. (...) So I would advise always, a serious questioning of any message, particularly those containing 'forecasts' of the future."[84]

As a final clue, when a message appeals to selfish desires, such as aiming for a certain status, even for spiritual advancement, we may be sure that the source is of a similarly 'coloured' level. Therefore, Benjamin Creme suggests we use our intuition when trying to establish from which level messages originate: "Intuition comes from the heart and has nothing to do with the desire principle which is astral and comes from the solar plexus. Try to realize the difference between these two..."[85]

Notes

1   Benjamin Creme's Master (1998), 'The New Age is upon us'. In: Creme (ed., 2004), *A Master speaks*, 3rd expanded edition, p.341
2   Alice A. Bailey (1951), *A Treatise on the Seven Rays, Vol. III – Esoteric Astrology*, 10th printing 1975, pp.472-73
3   George Adamski (1955), *Inside the Space Ships*, pp.94-95
4   Enrique Barrios (1989), *Ami, Child of the Stars*, pp.36-37
5   Adamski (1955), op cit, pp.201-02
6   Howard Menger (1959), *From Outer Space to You*, p.47
7   Daniel Fry, (1954a), *[A Report By Alan] To Men of Earth*, in Fry (1966), *The White Sands Incident*, pp.77-78
8   Ibidem, pp.78-79
9   Barrios (1989), op cit, p.84
10 Adamski (1955), op cit, p.139
11 Fry (1954a), op cit, p.90
12 Ibid., op cit, p.91
13 Adamski (1955), op cit, pp.137-38
14 Fry (1954a), op cit, pp.73-74
15 Ibid., op cit, p.74
16 Adamski (1957-58), *Cosmic Science for the Promotion of Cosmic Principles and Truth* – Series No. 1, Part No.2, Question #25
17 Fry (1954a), op cit, pp.75-76
18 Adamski (1957-58), op cit, Part No.2, Question #23
19 Ibid., Part No.4, Question #72
20 Peter Senge et al (2004), *Presence – Human Purpose and the Field of the Future*, p.14
21 Adamski (1955), op cit, pp.88-89

22 Benjamin Creme's Master (2014), 'Problems awaiting action'. *Share International* magazine, Vol.33, No.3, April, p.3

23 Bailey (1957), *The Externalization of the Hierarchy*, p.580

24 Stephen Leahy (2013), 'Building a better world, one block at a time'. Inter Press Service News Agency [online], 8 October. Available at <www.ipsnews.net/2013/10/building-a-better-world-one-block-at-a-time/>. [Accessed 5 August 2015]

25 Source: www.transitionnetwork.org

26 Niels Bos (2014), 'Our changing view of food: from commodity to commons'. *Share International* magazine, Vol.33, No.4, May, pp.17-18, 20

27 Thiago Staibano Alves (2014), 'Business without bosses – democracy in the workplace'. *Share International* magazine, Vol.33, No.3, April, pp.17-18

28 Source: www.johnlewispartnership.co.uk/

29 Source: PayScale. See www.payscale.com/data-packages/ceo-income [Accessed 8 August 2015]

30 Paul Mason (2015), 'The end of capitalism has begun'. *The Guardian* [online], 17 July. Available at <www.theguardian.com/books/2015/jul/17/postcapitalism-end-of-capitalism-begun>. [Accessed 18 July 2015]

31 Stefan Denaerde (1977), *Operation Survival Earth*, p.61

32 Tex Gunning (2011), 'Value Based Education'. NIVOZ lecture, 13 October. Available at <hetkind.org/wp-content/uploads/2011/10/Value-Based-Education-lezing-Tex-Gunning-13-oktober-2011-NIVOZ.pdf>

33 Creme (2012), *Unity in Diversity – The Way Ahead for Humanity*, p.82

34 Creme (2014), 'Questions and answers'. *Share International* magazine, Vol.33, No.5, June, p.22

35 Barrios (1989), op cit, pp.99-100

36 Creme (2012), op cit, p.90

37 Bailey (1957), op cit, pp.580-81

38 Creme (2012), op cit, p.79

39 Creme (2013), 'Questions and answers'. *Share International* magazine, Vol.32, No.10, December, p.23

40 Benjamin Creme's Master (2012), 'The Great Decision'. *Share International* magazine, Vol.31, No.1, January/February, p.3

41 Adamski (1957-58), op cit, Part No.3, Question #44

42 Adamski (1955), op cit, p.117

43 Adamski (1957-58), op cit, Part No.4, Question #80

44 Adamski (1955), op cit, pp.239-40

45 Adamski (1957-58), op cit, Part No.3, Question #49

46 Roberto Savio (2013), 'Switzerland Sets Example for Income Equality'. Inter Press Service News Agency [online], 11 March. Available at <www.ipsnews.net/2013/03/switzerland-sets-example-for-income-equality/>. [Accessed 5 August 2015]

47 Denaerde (1977), op cit, pp.114-15
48 Creme (2012), op cit, pp. 21-22
49 Benjamin Creme's Master (1994), 'To serve anew'. In: Creme (ed.;
    2004), *A Master Speaks*, 3rd expanded edition, p.257
50 Denaerde (1977), op cit, p.132
51 Fry (1954a), op cit, p.84
52 Truman Bethurum (1954), *Aboard a Flying Saucer*, pp.74-75
53 Adamski (1957-58), op cit, Part No.2, Question #39
54 Fry (1954a), op cit, p.92
55 Wilbert Smith (1969), *The Boys from Topside*, p.29
56 Ibid., p.28
57 Adamski (1955), op cit, p.93
58 Benjamin Creme's Master (1999), 'The Blueprint of the Future'. In:
    Creme (ed.; 2004), op cit, p.359
59 Creme (2010), *The Gathering of the Forces of Light – UFOs and their Spiritual
    Mission*, p.37
60 Adamski (1955), op cit, p.100
61 Barrios (1989), op cit, p.87
62 Adamski (1955), op cit, p.184
63 Fry (1954a), op cit, pp.70-71
64 Adamski (1936), *Wisdom of the Masters of the Far East*, p.33
65 Fry (1954a), op cit, p.71

The message and the source

66 Adamski (1955), op cit, p.222
67 Adamski (1965), *Answers to Questions Most Frequently Asked About the
    Space Visitors and Life on Other Planets* , p.15
68 Ibid., p.21
69 Aartsen (2010), *George Adamski – A Herald for the Space Brothers*, 2nd ed.
    2012, pp.20-23
70 Creme (2001), op cit, p.76
71 Creme (1993), *Maitreya's Mission, Vol. Two*, pp.565-66
72 Adamski (1962), 'World Disturbances'. In: *Cosmic Science*, Vol.1, No.1,
    January 1962, p.4
73 Adamski (1957-58), op cit, Part No.1, Question #14
74 Adamski (1955), op cit, p.99
75 Barrios (1989), op cit, p.33
76 Ibid., p.99
77 Ibid., p.33
78 Adamski (1955), op cit, p.104
79 Menger (1959), op cit, p.37
80 Creme (2001), op cit, p.28

81 Bailey (1948), *The Reappearance of the Christ*, p.74
82 Creme (2001), op cit, p.9
83 Adamski (1957-58), op cit, Part No.5, Question #85
84 Ibid., Part No.1, Question #15
85 Creme (2014), 'Questions and answers'. *Share International* magazine, Vol.33, No.2, March, p.26

Planets as school rooms in the Cosmos (pp.149-50)

a Eileen Buckle (1967), *The Scoriton Mystery – Did Adamski Return?*, pp.61-63
b Giorgio Dibitonto (1990), *Angels in Starships*, p.30
c Wendelle C. Stevens (1990), Preface in Dibitonto (1990), op cit
d Gennady Belimov, 'Boriska – Boy from Mars'. *Pravda* [online], 12 March 2004. Available at <web.archive.org/web/20040402081230/ english.pravda.ru/science/19/94/377/12257_Martian.html>. [Accessed 14 August 2015]
e Creme (ed., 2005), 'Signs of the time'. *Share International* magazine, Vol.24, No.7, September, p.16
f See, for instance, Creme (1993), *Maitreya's Mission, Vol. Two*, p.553 and (2010), *The Gathering of the Forces of Light – UFOs and their Spiritual Mission*, p.40

Epilogue

On the cover of my previous book I summarized the general message as conveyed through the contactees of the 1950s and their successors as: "Life is One, so live as one, or perish…" In this book, I have shown how the space people have given us glimpses of the way they have organised life on their planets as a practical expression of the Oneness to which all great Teachers of humanity have testified, and which we have ignored at our peril.

While *Here to Help* shows how the extraterrestrial presence is ultimately and intricately connected with the next step in the evolution of human consciousness, *Priorities for a Planet in Transition – The Space Brothers' Case for Justice and Freedom* continues where the previous book left off and presents the reader with an unprecedented compilation of evidence that the space visitors have not just been reminding us of the need to reconnect with our spiritual origins, but have actually shown us numerous examples of how life may be organised differently for lasting peace and prosperity for all.

What started as the 'flying saucer movement' and evolved into 'ufology', is now often referred to as 'exopolitics', in an attempt to lend academic credence to a topic that has suffered so much from secrecy and disinformation.

The simplest definition of 'exopolitics' at the moment goes something like: "The study of the political actors, processes and institutions associated with extraterrestrial life", to allow for the many conflicting theories about the intentions of the extra-terrestrial visitors. Also, for some this definition presupposes the existence of extraterrestrial life, for others merely the possibility of such.

However, based on the body of evidence in this book, and its pertinence to the state of the world today, a far more practical and evidence-based definition of the term 'exopolitics' presents itself, which goes back to the original meaning of its constituents, with 'exo' meaning "(from) outside" and 'politics' meaning "matters concerning the state or its citizens":

Exopolitics – People from other planets showing humanity alternative, saner ways of organising society, without imposing their views.

This makes 'exopolitics' at once a much more urgent concept and places the extraterrestrial presence on Earth solidly in the context of the crises facing humanity today – political, economic, financial, social and environmental.

In my previous books I inevitably touched on the socio-economic implications of giving expression to our Oneness with one and All. Seeing the amount of information that the Space Brothers have shared with us in this respect, ranging from seemingly off-the-cuff remarks to a two-day exposé of their planets' social and economic organisation, as well as actual visits, is truly astounding, as it presents us with a comprehensive picture of how life on their planets has been organised for sustainability, and freedom and justice for all.

As such, it provides a much needed and hope-inspiring example of how it could be with us.

APPENDICES

I. The research method: A critical synthesis

Given that the history of the modern UFO era, starting after World War II, is fraught with cover-ups, disinformation, conspiracy theories, speculation and attention-seeking, hardly anyone knows what information to trust or take seriously. As a result, despite massive amounts of evidence, countless reliable sightings and a wealth of eyewitness testimonies, a majority of people – and especially the media – do not even take the subject of extraterrestrial visits seriously.

No doubt this majority will catch up as irrefutable events unfold, but for those who are currently wrestling to identify authentic information I contend that there is really no need to "believe". Instead, I suggest, there is a viable way to establish fact from fiction or deliberate falsehood. Because of the nature of the extraterrestrial presence so far, this isn't as straightforward as taking measurements and compiling and analysing the data thus obtained. Most experiences and statements are subjective and cannot be repeated, however much desired by many, as in laboratory experiments.

In the Gospel according to Matthew we read, "Seek and ye shall find." Unfortunately, Matthew forgot to add that typically, what we will find depends on what we seek. So if researchers are looking for accounts that claim the extraterrestrial presence is a threat, they will find them, just as there are piles of accounts to the contrary. How then do we decide whose testimony is credible?

In his 'baloney detection kit' the esteemed Carl Sagan said: "If whatever it is you're explaining has some measure, some numerical quantity attached to it, you'll be much better able to discriminate among competing hypotheses. What is vague and qualitative is open to many explanations. Of course there are truths to be sought in the many qualitative issues we are obliged to confront, but finding *them* is more challenging."[1] The challenge, therefore, is to devise an acceptable approach to qualitative research in this field to establish that which cannot be measured or established by quantitative or reductionist methods.

In the late 1950s Canadian engineer and researcher Wilbert Smith reported: "In several instances reliable people have reported seeing the beings who ride about on these craft, and they say they look just like us. There are quite a number of reported contacts between these people from elsewhere and people of Earth (...) and the results of these contacts are remarkably consistent and enlightening."[2] In an article from 1958, he described his research as follows: "The procedure in checking contacts was to ask a number of innocuous but significant questions and compare the answers with the answers to the same questions as obtained through other contacts. Questions were of the type: Do people live on the planet Mars? If so, what is the general shape of their houses? Do people on Mars use coinage money? If so, what does it look like? All together some hundred or more questions were involved. The results were spectacular to say the least. Among the contacts that might be classed as authentic there was almost complete agreement. Among the other alleged contacts there was extremely poor agreement, or none at all. Of course where agreement was general, but one or two points didn't fit in, an effort was made to find out the reason for the discrepancy. In each case it was found that someone had injected a terrestrial idea or comment, frequently of a religious nature, instead of transmitting faithfully that what was received."[3]

The research method I have employed is very similar to the procedure described here by Wilbert Smith and helps to sift through contact claims by looking at specific information from independent sources, in order to obtain data about such "qualitative issues" that "we are obliged to confront" in the face of so much disinformation and ignorance.

Given the multitude of conflicting theories and reports it is essential to establish some basic criteria that may serve as parameters or touchstones against which to test the validity of any claim of extraterrestrial contact – voluntary or involuntary alike. In order to do this we will look for these facts from the neutral thesis that – because of conflicting reports – many people are unsure if the extraterrestrial visitors are benign, oppressive, or perhaps both. And, given that disinformation is seen as one of the most important obstacles to establishing what is real, the obvious point to start from are the reports that we know were *not* contaminated by disinformation, misinformation and speculation. The fact that these are many and originate from different parts of the world ensures our criteria will be universal, reliable and usable.

1. Historical considerations

Since there are so many hypotheses about the extraterrestrial presence we need to start our inquiry at the beginning of the history of the modern UFO era, with the many reported sightings of 'foo fighters' by fighter pilots during World War II, the sighting by Kenneth Arnold in June 1947, the crash (some would say 'alleged') of a saucer near Roswell in July 1947, and the experiences of the contactees of the early 1950s which led to a truly worldwide frenzy of public attention. About speculation that flying saucers might be of terrestrial origin, Desmond Leslie argued in his inimitably cheerful manner, "…the only objection to the 'Alien [i.e. enemy] Power Theory' is that these saucers have been flying all over the world (of friend and foe alike) for rather a long time. Researches show that they appeared in large numbers and were seen by eminent astronomers years before the Wright Brothers had made their first successful heavier-than-air flight. In that case, any earthly power which had them in its possession must be of a very peaceable nature, for it could have conquered the world, practically overnight, any time it so chose."[4]

Strikingly, these early sightings and experiences were either neutral or decidedly friendly. Also, the fact that there have been no reports from WWII fighter pilots about aggression, or reports from the original contactees about 'abductions', indicates a neutral or friendly presence.

If we are visited by extraterrestrials with both good and bad intentions, there is no reason why contact of only one type should have happened without that of the other type happening during the time of the first reported contacts.

2. <u>Social considerations</u>

Contacts, which began to reach the public in the early 1950s, were first reported by people with little to no formal education and no particular societal 'status', such as Buck Nelson, Truman Bethurum, Orfeo Angelucci, and George Adamski. Later, reports from people with higher levels of education, such as Daniel Fry, Wilbert Smith and Dino Kraspedon, were published. Now, in 2015, we have reports from people in the military, astronauts, scientists and even government/diplomats who testify, based on their personal experiences, of the friendly intentions of the visitors. There are no reports from any such dignitaries of having been 'abducted' or subjected to any of the atrocities that are now often ascribed to the visitors. **If we are visited by extraterrestrials with both good and bad intentions, there is no reason why one type of contact would happen only to people from one section of society experiencing contact, and not from other social strata.**

3. Political considerations
When the first contacts were reported, the world was deeply divided (West vs East) and under severe threat of nuclear annihilation. Most contactees were asked to warn the world of these dangers and to stress the need for worldwide co-operation to avert disaster, with reported offers to help us with alternative technology if humanity would abolish nuclear technology. (Adamski's one-time co-author Desmond Leslie was among the early members of the Campaign for Nuclear Disarmament, CND in the UK.[5]) Being gravely concerned about the massive public interest in this hopeful message of international brotherhood and peace, the political, military and corporate establishments started a concerted disinformation campaign to scare and confuse the public.[6] Later contactees, such as Giorgio Dibitonto, during his experiences in 1980[7], also received severe warnings about the dangers of nuclear technology.

Likewise, the information from the early contactees coincides 100 per cent with the political consensus about the emergency actions to be taken to solve Earth's problems and prevent catastrophy, as expressed in the Brandt Commission report (see page 110). **If we are visited by extraterrestrials with both good and bad intentions, we should have reports of authentic contacts promoting not only co-operation, justice, and peace but also the opposite, as well as offers for further destructive technology from contacts at any given time since the early 1950s.**

4. Spiritual considerations
The messages and information coming from both the original and many later contactees are imbued with the same notions of respect for humanity's free will, the expansion of consciousness and the Golden Rule as we find in the Ageless Wisdom teaching of Earth, while to some extent they also share the latter two with the world's major religions.

If we are visited by extraterrestrials with both good and bad intentions, we should have reports of life philosophies or teachings from authentic contacts that not only coincide with or confirm the basic teachings of humanity's shared wisdom traditions and religions, but with opposing teachings or views on life as well.

Having established these facts, we can now use them as criteria to test claims of any kind of contact and decide for ourselves if they pass the test of these historical, social, political and spiritual considerations, without which, we can see, they will go against substantiated evidence, logic and common sense. If contact claims do not stand up to the criteria we have established, we need to see whether there is evidence to the contrary or if there are alternative explanations.

As an example, let's take the claim of 'abduction' in general and see how it holds up to the facts that we have established.
(1) None of the early contactees have reported being taken against their will, or their (physical) integrity being violated in any way, other than the occasional scratch or burn due to unfamiliarity with a craft's force field.
(2) There have been no reports among officials and dignitaries who have gone on the record about their personal experiences of 'abductions' or having been subjected to 'experiments'.
(3) There are no reports of people who claim to have been told

that (nuclear) war would be an option.

(4) There are no reports of people having had contact who have been offered details or understanding of a 'materialistic' or 'self-ish' view of life, say, for instance, a Nazi-like philosophy.

Since the claim of 'abduction' does not stand up to scrutiny against our authentic contact criteria, yet thousands of people claim to have had an 'abduction' experience of some kind, we must establish if there is a valid alternative explanation for such experiences. In fact, there are at least four plausible explanations:

(a) First of all, a number of people who say they have been 'abducted' may simply be employing the terminology in the usually indiscriminate or sensationalist reporting on these matters to describe a 'regular' contact experience.

(b) Given that there is documentary evidence that vested interests have attempted to scare and confuse the public about the extraterrestrial presence, 'abduction' experiences may be staged by secret operatives. In fact, researchers have found evidence of 'black budgets' which could be used towards staging such false experiences, and in 2006 Steven Greer claimed that numerous witnesses have testified to such activities[8], often referred to as MILABS (military abductions) and Unacknowledged Special Access Projects (USAPs). Implanting or erasing memories by means of drugs, hypnosis or a combination, has been an aspect of psychological warfare for many decades.

(c) Over time, a massive and powerful thoughtform has built up from humanity's dreams and fears. Because the majority of people are astrally polarized (i.e. in the solar plexus), these thoughtforms are readily tapped into while daydreaming (see pages 153-57) and people convince themselves that their experiences are real. These can vary from receiving 'guidance' from 'archangels' to being 'abducted by aliens' or worse, and everything in between.

(d) People who claim to have been 'abducted' may have simply experienced it as a result of overactive (astral) imagination, for any number of possible psychological reasons. There are many well-known cases of 'experiences' being contageous or people 'taking on' experiences of others, such as mysterious cases of people falling asleep or ill for no apparent reason, or hearing sounds, or seeing things. As George Adamski once said about such experiences: "To them they are real ... but so are dreams to the dreamer."[9]

Now let us see if we can test our parameters on an example that goes beyond personal contact, namely the claim that governments or shadier powers on Earth have succeeded in back-engineering anti-gravity and other extraterrestrial technology in collusion with nefarious 'aliens', which they keep a secret from the rest of us and are using to control humanity and the planet – according to some speculations, operating from bases on the moon and Mars. (There are more than a few people who are convinced that this is what is going on, and perhaps it is helpful for some to see the utter lack of logic in such speculations.) We will apply our four parameters as in the order above.

(1) Historically, the contactees have stated, almost without exception, that a certain level of moral development, a certain stage in the evolution of consciousness which entails a definite sense of its oneness, has to be reached before a planetary race will be able (allowed, even) to develop the technology needed to travel around the solar system. Without such moral development, technological advances beyond a certain point will turn themselves against such a race. To wit, after a period of détente, today we are again facing the dangers of technological advancement paired

with a lack of fundamental ethics on Earth.

(2) Claims of this kind are often backed up with testimonies from people who have worked, or claim to have worked, at secret bases, sometimes allegedly in cooperation with extra-terrestrials. Given the lengths that governments and the military have gone to in order to confuse and scare the public, it is impossible to know to what extent their experiences are factual or implanted memories, or mixed with further misinformation.

There is also the much cited claim by the late Lockheed Skunk Works engineer Ben Rich: "We now have the technology to take ET home." But military aviation historian Peter Merlin, who attendend many of his talks, explains that this statement was merely misconstrued from a successful tagline which Mr Rich used at the end of his talks since 1983: "The Skunk Works has been assigned the task of getting [the movie character] E.T. back home."[10] (See also the statements made by astronaut Dr Edgar Mitchell and esotericist Benjamin Creme in this respect on page 39.)

(3) As for the political criterion, the claim that we are assessing here, in any of its forms that allege the deployment of these secret technologies to control humanity and the planet, is illogical in that the very elite that is supposed to keep these technologies secret already own most of the planet and its resources.

(4) It should be clear that the human race, and certainly the elite that is alleged to be in possession of the means to travel around the solar system, has not yet reached the point in evolution (see 1) necessary to do so.

Many readers will be familiar with the term 'critical analysis' as an analytical evaluation of an idea or a text and its validity. An analysis answers questions about the author, the nature of his work that is under consideration, his thesis, how it relates to other material on the same subject, his evidence, et cetera, all of which lead to a conclusion.

By checking claims of contact from multiple authors against the criteria established above, we can collect qualitative data substantiated by correspondences with historical sources, and corroboration from independent sources over time, social classes and different backgrounds, such as for instance, science, military, politics, religion, and the wisdom teachings.

As long as government and military files are going to remain classified we will be left without tangible evidence. The more so, given the Space Brothers' efforts to respect our free will and freedom of thought. Yet, as it is based on qualitative research of primary sources, this method provides us with four criteria that allow us to test any other contact claim since the 1950s:

1) **The historical criterion**: Authentic contact coincides with the benign nature of the original contacts.
2) **The social criterion**: Authentic contact occurs across all social strata.
3) **The political criterion**: Authentic contact promotes right human relations through cooperation, justice, freedom and peace, and environmental awareness.
4) **The spiritual criterion**: Authentic contact testifies to respect for humanity's free will, growth of consciousness, and the Golden Rule.

Synthesizing the information that we have scrutinized in this way, a vivid and sweeping picture emerges not only of life on other planets but, more importantly, of how we may use the examples that we have been shown to our advantage, in order to secure a peaceful and prosperous future for all. Readers will also find that this approach exposes the tales of 'aliens' perpetrating terror on Earth as merely another demon of the type that Carl Sagan's book *The Demon-Haunted World* was designed to expunge by quantitative means.

Taking the pre-disinformation accounts as its primary yardstick, this research method also incorporates logic and common sense, and goes beyond the meme (paraphrased): "I want to believe... anything" which, I suggest, is not being open-minded, but simply being uncritical, and ignores the definite touchstones for validity that we do have.

Those who look for claims that confirm their fears, will find them in abundance. But readers who are looking for verifiable and substantiated information that, from the start, has called on us to play an active part in the crisis which humanity is presently going through and thereby inspires hope for the future, should now have the means for qualitative research that cuts through disinformation, misinformation and speculation.

Notes

1   Carl Sagan (1997), *The Demon-Haunted World*, pp.196-97
2   Wilbert Smith (1969), *The Boys from Topside*, p.21
3   Smith (1958), 'Why I believe in the Reality of Spacecraft'. *Flying Saucer Review*, Vol.4, No.6, November-December, p.9
4   Desmond Leslie (1955), 'Astronomy and Space-Men', *Flying Saucer Review*, Vol.1, No.3, July-August, p.23
5   Robert O'Byrne (2010), *Desmond Leslie (1921-2001) – The Biography of an Irish Gentleman*, p.102
6   See Gerard Aartsen (2011), *Here to Help: UFOs and the Space Brothers*, Chapter 2, and the current volume, pp.10-11
7   See Giorgio Dibitonto (1990), *Angels in Starships*.
8   Steven Greer (2006), 'The Disclosure Project, [online] 2 May. Available at <www.disclosureproject.org/docs/pdf/ExopoliticsOrXenopolitics.pdf> [Accessed 11 July 2015]
9   George Adamski (1957-58), *Cosmic Science for the Promotion of Cosmic Principles and Truth*, Series No.1, Part No.5, Question #88
10 Peter R. Merlin (2013), 'Taking ET home: The birth of a modern myth'. *SUNlite*, Vol.5, No.6, November-December, pp.17-19. [Accessed 7 April 2015]

II. The Golden Rule
(The Law of Harmlessness)
as expressed in various religious traditions

Baha'i
"Lay not on any soul a load that you would not wish to be laid upon you, and desire not for anyone the things you would not desire for yourself." –*Baha'u'llah, Gleanings*

Buddhism
"Treat not others in ways that you yourself would find hurtful." –*Gautama Buddha, Udana-Varga 5:18*

Confucianism
"Do not do to others what you do not want done to yourself." –*Confucius, Analects 15.23*

Christianity
"Therefore all things whatsoever ye would that men should do to you, do ye even so to them: for this is the law and the prophets." –*Jesus, Matthew 7:12*

Hinduism
"One should never do that to another which one regards as injurious to one's own self. This, in brief, is the rule of Righteousness." –*Mahabharata, Anusasana Parva 113.8*

Islam
"Not one of you truly believes until you wish for your brothers what you wish for yourself." –*the Prophet Muhammad, Forty Hadith of an-Nawawi 13*

Jainism

"One should treat all creatures in the world as one would like to be treated." *–Mahavira, Sutrakritanga 1.11.33*

Judaism

"What is hateful to you, do not do to your neighbor. This is the whole Law; all the rest is commentary." *–Hillel, Talmud, Shabbat 31a*

Native American

"Do not wrong or hate your neighbor. For it is not he who you wrong, but yourself." *–Pima proverb*

Sikhism

"I am a stranger to no one; and no one is a stranger to me. Indeed, I am a friend to all." *–Guru Granth Sahib, p.1299*

Taoism

"Regard your neighbour's gain as your own gain, and your neighbour's loss as your own loss." *–T'ai Shang Kan Ying P'ien, 213-218*

Wicca

"An it harm none, do what ye will." *–Wiccan Rede*

Zoroastrianism

"Whatever is disagreeable to yourself, do not do unto others." *–Shayast-na-Shayast 13:29*

Sources and references

BBC London, ' "UFO" spotted over London 2012 site', 10 November 2009

Der Bund, 'Es leuchtete und schwebte über das Weserstadion', 9 January 2014

Castanet website, 'Castanet's UFO? video', 13 August 2014

China.org.cn, 'Second UFO seen over Chongqing', 16 July 2010

CrypticMedia, 'UFO Over Chicago O'Hare', 30 August 2007

English Eastday, 'Mystery of glowing white ball in the sky', 23 August 2011

The Guardian, 'Unbridled capitalism is the "dung of the devil", says Pope Francis', 10 July 2015

InfoBAE.com, 'Misterio "cósmico" en San Lorenzo: ¿un OVNI sobrevoló el "Nuevo Gasómetro"?', 22 April 2014

Oxfam, 'Richest 1% will own more than all the rest by 2016', 19 January 2015

The Siberian Times, 'So did a UFO shoot down the famous Chelyabinsk meteorite last month?', 28 February 2013

The Sydney Morning Herald, 'Bright lights on dwarf planet Ceres perplex NASA scientists', 27 February 2015

Tazi Sutrin, BTV, interview with Lachezar Filipov, Bulgaria, October 2012

The Telegraph, 'Aliens "already exist on earth", Bulgarian scientists claim', 26 November 2009

Todas Noticias, 'Viralísimo: el mundo habla de un "ovni" que apareció al aire en TN', 6 March 2015

Trading Economics, 'Spain Youth Unemployment Rate', 14 April 2014

UFO Evidence, 'Two children encounter UFO and small humanoid beings in Cussac, France', n.d.

UFO Sightings Hotspot blog, 'Huge UFO spotted on SOHO image', 1 March, 2015

United Nations Organisation, 'The Universal Declaration of Human Rights', 1948

The White House Office of the Press Secretary, 'President Barack Obama's State of the Union Address', 28 January 2014

Wikipedia, 'James E. McDonald', n.d.

World Economic Forum, *Outlook on the Global Agenda 2014,* Chapter 2, 'Widening income disparities', 2014

Gerard Aartsen. 'End the UFO/ET disclosure nonsense!' (Netherlands, Amsterdam: BGA Publications YouTube video, 2015)

Gerard Aartsen. *George Adamski – A Herald for the Space Brothers.* (Netherlands, Amsterdam: BGA Publications, 2010)

Gerard Aartsen. *Here to Help: UFOs and the Space Brothers.* (Netherlands, Amsterdam: BGA Publications, 2011), 2nd expanded edition, 2012

SOURCES AND REFERENCES

Gerard Aartsen. *Our Elder Brothers Return – A History in Books*. (Netherlands, Amsterdam: BGA Publications, 2008); published online at www.biblioteca-ga.info

George Adamski. *Answers to Questions Most Frequently Asked About Our Space Visitors and Other Planets*. (USA, Palomar Gardens, CA: G. Adamski, 1965)

George Adamski. *Cosmic Bulletin*. (USA, Valley Center, CA: The Adamski Foundation, 1965)

George Adamski. *Cosmic Science for the Promotion of Cosmic Principles and Truths*. (USA, Valley Center, CA: Cosmic Science, 1957-58)

George Adamski. *Flying Saucers Farewell*. (USA, New York, NY: Abelard-Schuman, 1961)

George Adamski. *Inside the Space Ships*. (USA, New York, NY: Abelard-Schumann, 1955)

George Adamski. 'The Space People' (1964). In: Gerard Aartsen, *George Adamski – A Herald for the Space Brothers*, 2010

George Adamski. *Special Report: My Trip to the Twelve Counsellors' Meeting That Took Place on Saturn, March 27-30, 1962*. (USA, Vista, CA: Science of Life, 1962)

George Adamski. *Wisdom of the Masters of the Far East*. Facsimile reprint (USA, CA, Mokelumne Hill: Health Research, 1974)

George Adamski. 'World Disturbances'. In: *Cosmic Science*, Vol.1, No.1, January 1962

Stéphane Allix (dir). *Experiencers*. (France: 13E Rue, 2011)

Thiago Staibano Alves. 'Business without bosses – democracy in the workplace'. *Share International* magazine, Vol.33, No.3, April 2014

Orfeo Angelucci. *The Secret of the Saucers*. (USA, Amherst, WI: The Amherst Press, 1955)

Alice A. Bailey. *The Externalisation of the Hierarchy*. (UK, London: Lucis Trust, 1957)

Alice A. Bailey. *The Reappearance of the Christ*. (UK, London: Lucis Trust, 1948), 5th printing, 1969

Alice A. Bailey. *A Treatise on the Seven Rays, Vol. III – Esoteric Astrology*. (UK, London: Lucis Trust, 1951), 10th printing 1975

Alice A. Bailey. *A Treatise on the Seven Rays, Vol. V – Esoteric Healing*. (UK, London: Lucis Trust, 1953), 5th printing, 1970

Eliza Barclay. 'More cities are making it illegal to hand out food to the homeless'. NPR *The Salt*, 22 October 2014

Enrique Barrios. *Ami, Child of the Stars*. (USA, Santa Fe, NM: Lotus Press, 1989)

Gennady Belimov. 'Boriska – Boy from Mars'. *Pravda*, 12 March 2004

Truman Bethurum. *Aboard a Flying Saucer*. (USA, Los Angeles, CA: DeVorss & Co., 1954)

Willy Brandt (ed). *North-South – A Programme for Survival*. (USA, Cambridge, MA: The MIT Press/UK, London: Pan Books, 1980)

Niels Bos. 'Our changing view of food: from commodity to commons'. *Share International* magazine, Vol.33, No.4, May 2014

Stefano Breccia. *Mass Contacts*. (UK, Milton Keynes: AuthorHouse, 2009)

Eileen Buckle. *The Scoriton Mystery – Did Adamski Return?* (UK, London: Neville Spearman, 1967)

Andrew Buncombe. 'US Presidential aide John Podesta says biggest regret is not securing release of government records about UFOs'. *The Independent*, 16 February 2015

Norman Byrd. 'UFO caught "monitoring" International Space Station on live camera'. Examiner.com, 9 October 2014

Joseph A. Califano Jr. 'What Was Really Great About The Great Society – The truth behind the conservative myths', *The Washington Monthly*, October 1999

Robert Chapman. *UFO – Flying Saucers over Britain?* (UK, Frogmore, St Albans, Herts: Mayflower Books Ltd, 1972), 1974 reprint

Stephen Coan. 'The day the aliens landed'. *The Witness*, 16 April 2008

Steve Connor. 'The galaxy collisions that shed light on unseen parallel Universe'. *The Independent*, 26 March 2015

David Crary and Lisa Leff. 'Number of Homeless Children in America Surges to All-Time High: Report'. *The Huffington Post*, 17 November 2014

Benjamin Creme. *The Art of Cooperation*. (USA, Los Angeles, CA: Share International, 2002)

Benjamin Creme. *The Gathering of the Forces of Light – UFOs and their Spiritual Mission*. (USA, Los Angeles, CA: Share International, 2010)

Benjamin Creme. *The Great Approach – New Light and Life for Humanity*. (USA, Los Angeles, CA: Share International, 2001)

Benjamin Creme. *Maitreya's Mission, Vol. Two*. (USA, Los Angeles, CA: Share International, 1993)

Benjamin Creme. *Maitreya's Mission, Vol. Three*. (USA, Los Angeles, CA: Share International, 1997)

Benjamin Creme. *The Reappearance of the Christ and the Masters of Wisdom*. (UK, London: Tara Press, 1979)

Benjamin Creme. *Unity in Diversity – The Way Ahead for Humanity*. (USA, Los Angeles, CA: Share International, 2012)

Benjamin Creme (ed). *A Master Speaks*, 3rd expanded edition. (USA, Los Angeles, CA: Share International, 2004)

Benjamin Creme (ed). *Maitreya's Teachings – The Laws of Life*. (USA, Los Angeles, CA: Share International, 2005)

Benjamin Creme (ed). *Messages from Maitreya the Christ*. (USA, Los Angeles, CA: Tara Press, 1992)

SOURCES AND REFERENCES

Benjamin Creme (ed). *Share International* magazine Vol.8, No.3, April 1989; Vol.22, No.5, May 2003; Vol.24, No.7, September 2005; Vol.26, No.1, January/February 2007; Vol.28, No.1, January/February 2009; Vol.28, No.11, November 2009; Vol.30, No.8, October 2011; Vol.31, No.7, September 2012; Vol.32, No.3, April 2013; Vol.32, No.7, September 2013; Vol.32, No.10, December 2013; Vol.33, No.2, March 2014; Vol.33, No.5, June 2014; Vol.33, No.6, July/August 2014

Stefan Denaerde. *Contact from Planet Iarga*. (USA, Tucson, AZ: UFO Photo Archives, 1982)

Stefan Denaerde. *Operation Survival Earth*. (USA, New York, NY: Simon & Schuster Pocket Books, 1977)

Giorgio Dibitonto. *Angels in Starships*. (USA, Phoenix, AZ: UFO Photo Archives, 1990)

Christopher Donato. '90-Year-old man charged with feeding the homeless says he won't give up'. ABC News, 6 November 2014

Natalie Evans. 'UF-Olympics? "Alien spacecraft" caught on camera over the London 2012 opening ceremony'. *Daily Mirror*, 31 July 2012

Siobhan Fenton. 'Welfare cuts: Statistics watchdog urges Government to release clear information on benefits sanctions'. *The Independent*, 8 August 2015

Carlos Fredo. 'OVNI sobre el volcán Popocatépetl, octubre 2012'. StarMedia, 2 November 2012

Daniel Fry. *Alan's Message: To Men of Earth* (1954). As reprinted in: Daniel Fry. *The White Sands Incident*. (USA, Louisville, KY: Best Books Inc, 1966)

Daniel Fry. *The White Sands Incident*. (USA, Los Angeles, CA: New Age Publishing, 1954)

Amelia Gentleman. ' "No one should die penniless and alone": the victims of Britain's harsh welfare sanctions'. *The Guardian*, 3 August 2014

Waveney Girvan. 'The Adamski Photographs – an open challenge'. *Flying Saucer Review*, Vol 6, No.2, March-April 1960

Waveney Girvan. Letter to the Editor, *The Observer*, 25 October 1955

Timothy Good. *Alien Base – Earth's Encounters with Extraterrestrials*. (UK, London: Century, 1998)

Timothy Good. *Unearthly Disclosure*. (UK, London: Century, 2000)

Steven Greer, M.D. 'Exopolitics or Xenopolitics'. The Disclosure Project, 2 May 2006

Tex Gunning. 'Value Based Education'. (Netherlands: NIVOZ lecture, 13 October 2011)

Paola Leopizzi Harris. *Connecting the Dots... Making Sense Of The UFO Phenomenon*. (USA, Bloomingdale, IN: AuthorHouse, 2008)

Michael Hesemann (dir). *UFOs: The Contacts – The Pioneers of Space*. (Dusseldorf, Germany: 2000 Film Productions, 1996)

Jon Hilkevitch. 'In the sky! A bird? A plane? A … UFO?'. *Chicago Tribune*, 7 January 2007

Cynthia Hind. 'The Children of Ariel School'. *UFO AfriNews*, No.11, Feb. 1995

Cynthia Hind. *UFOs – African Encounters*. (Zimbabwe, Salisbury: Gemini, 1982)

Owen Jones. 'It's socialism for the rich and capitalism for the rest of us in Britain'. *The Guardian*, 29 August 2014

Rosie Jones (dir.), *Westall '66: A Suburban UFO Mystery*. (Australia: Screen Australia, Film Victoria, Endangered Pictures, 2010)

Alfie Kohn. 'Caring Kids – The Role of Schools'. *Phi Delta Kappan*, March 1991

Dino Kraspedon. *My Contact With Flying Saucers*. (USA, New York, NY: The Citadel Press, 1959)

Stephen Leahy. 'Building a better world, one block at a time'. Inter Press Service News Agency, 8 October 2013

Desmond Leslie. 'Astronomy and Space-Men'. *Flying Saucer Review*, Vol.1, No.3, July-August 1955

Desmond Leslie. 'Foreword'. In: Adamski. *Inside the Space Ships* (USA, New York, NY: Abelard-Schumann, 1955)

Desmond Leslie and George Adamski. *Flying Saucers Have Landed*, Revised & Enlarged edition (UK, London: Neville Spearman, 1970)

Nick Margerrison. Interview with Dr Edgar Mitchell on *The Night Before*. (UK, Peterborough: Kerrang! Radio 23 July, 2008)

Roger Marsh. '1966: Michigan children discover landed UFO in local field'. MUFON Case No. 63749, 13 March 2015

Paul Mason. 'The end of capitalism has begun'. *The Guardian*, 17 July 2015

Benjamin Creme's Master. 'The Great Decision'. *Share International* magazine, Vol.31, No.1, January/February, 2012

Benjamin Creme's Master. 'Problems awaiting action'. *Share International* magazine, Vol.33, No.3, April 2014

James McDonald. Archival footage in: Rosie Jones (dir.; 2010), *Westall '66: A Suburban UFO Mystery*. (Australia: Screen Australia, Film Victoria, Endangered Pictures, 2010)

Dmitry Medvedev. Off-air comments made after an interview on Russian TV, 7 December 2012

James Meek. 'Sale of the century: the privatisation scam'. *The Guardian*, 22 August 2014

Howard Menger. *From Outer Space to You*. (USA, Clarksburg, VA: Saucerian Books, 1959)

Peter Merlin. "Taking ET home: The birth of a modern myth'. *SUNlite*, Vol.5, No.6, November-December 2013

Drishya Nair. 'Mass UFO Sighting: Thousands watch "UFO" Hovering in Brazilian Skies during Protests'. *International Business Times*, 20 June 2013

Minnie Nair. 'Mass UFO Sighting: Spaceship Shoots up Vertically during Hong Kong protests'. *International Business Times*, 3 October 2014

Buck Nelson. *My Trip to Mars, the Moon, and Venus*. (USA, Missouri: Quill Press Company, 1956)

Tineke de Nooij. *Tineke's paranormale wereld*. (Netherlands: RTL4 TV, 27 March 1996)

Jimmy Nsubuga. 'Does this mystery white light captured by Nasa's Curiosity rover suggest there's life on Mars?'. *Metro UK*, 8 April 2014

Robert O'Byrne. *Desmond Leslie (1921-2001) – The Biography of an Irish Gentleman*. (Ireland, Dublin: The Lilliput Press, 2010)

Hillary Ojeda. 'YouTube: Unidentified flying object recorded in Lima today'. *Peru This Week* (2015)

Richard Padula. 'The day UFOs stopped play'. BBC News, 24 October 2014

Alberto Perego. *L'aviazione di altri pianeti opera tra noi: rapporto agli italiani: 1943-1963.* (Italy, Rome: Centro Italiano Studi Aviazione Elettromagnetica Roma, 1963)

Alejandro Rojas. 'Protesters in Brazil film UFO while drone films protesters'. Open Minds, 20 June 2013

Michael Rundle. 'UFOs Outside the International Space Station: Why Do We Keep Seeing Them?'. *Huffington Post UK*, 26 January 2015

Mary-Ann Russon. 'Nasa's Curiosity Rover Captures "Cigar-Shaped" UFO Orbiting Mars'. *International Business Times*, 13 May 2014

Sophie Ryan. 'UFOs captured on film near Queenstown'. *The New Zealand Herald*, 14 May 2014

Carl Sagan. *The Demon-Haunted World*. (UK, London: Headline Book Publishing, 1997)

Roberto Savio. 'Switzerland Sets Example for Income Equality'. Inter Press Service News Agency, 11 March 2013

Peter Senge et al. *Presence – Human Purpose and the Field of the Future*. (USA, New York, NY: Crown Business, 2004)

'Shadowhawk'. Comments to 'Can anyone find the source for this quote from Ben Rich. Re: hidden technology'. Above Top Secret website, 21 and 22 August 2013

Wilbert Smith. *The Boys from Topside*. (USA, Clarksburg, VA: Saucerian Books, 1969)

Wilbert Smith. 'Why I believe in the Reality of Spacecraft'. *Flying Saucer Review*, Vol.4, No.6, November-December 1958

John Stevens. ' "UFOs" spotted over football stadium as Notre Dame game comes to a standstill'. Mail Online, 9 September 2011

Wendelle C. Stevens. 'Preface'. In: Georgio Dibitonto, *Angels in Starships*. (USA, Phoenix, AZ: UFO Photo Archives, 1990)

Megan Stewart. 'Nat Baily UFO now identified as Space Centre "hoax"'. *Vancouver Courier*, 10 September 2013

Marianne Szegedy-Maszak. '71 Years Ago FDR Dropped a Truthbomb That Still Resonates Today', *Mother Jones*, 12 April 2015

Giles Tremlett. 'The Podemos revolution: how a small group of radical academics changed European politics'. *The Guardian*, 31 March 2015

Claudia Urbaczka. 'UFO over German protest'. Letter to the editor. *Share International* magazine, Vol.31, No.1, January/February 2012

Joris Verhulst. 'February 15, 2003: The World Says No to War'. In: Stefaan Walgrave & Dieter Rucht (eds). *The world says no to war: Demonstrations against the War on Iraq*. (USA, Minneapolis, MN: University of Minnesota Press, 2010)

Arjun Walia. 'Amazing Footage: Thousands Witness UFO over Brazilian Protests'. *Collective Evolution*, 20 June 2013

Scott C. Waring. 'Dark UFO On Mars Caught by Curiosity Rover, July 2014'. UFO Sightings Daily, 18 July 2014

Scott C. Waring. 'US Presidents'. UFO Sightings Daily (n.d.)

H.G. Wells. *The New World Order.* The University of Adelaide Library web edition

Websites:
www.johnlewispartnership.co.uk
www.payscale.com/data-packages/ceo-income
www.transitionnetwork.org

Interview:
Mr Falco Friedhoff (Netherlands: Amsterdam, 4 April 2014)

INDEX

A

'Abduction' claims
  explanations for 171
Adamski, George
  4, 18, 42, 99, 170, 174
  about life on Venus 87
  about Mars 118
  claims cannot be dismissed 5
  Cosmic Science bulletin 4
  incarnated from Venus 149
  Inside the Space Ships 158
  mankind decides on change
    144
  on Cosmic Age 145
  ridiculed for talking about life
    on other planets 85
  space people have been
    coming here for centuries
    10
  space people not hostile 73
  visitors showed advanced way
    of life xi
  was aware of Law of Cyclic
    Appearance 43
  *Wisdom of the Masters of the
    Far East* 43
Advertising
  promotion of materialism
    63, 106
Ageless Wisdom teaching
  43, 172
  corroborated by information
    from contactees xi
  etheric planes of matter 85

Air Force
  actively suppressed UFO
    investigation 4
  Regulation 200-2, dated
    26 August 1953 4
Alternative energy
  blocked by fossil fuel industry
    67
Alves, Thiago Staibano 138
Amazing Mr Lutterworth, The 149
Ami, Child of the Stars
  6, 39, 100
Amicizia (Friendship) Case 10, 42
Angelucci, Orfeo 46, 170
Anti-gravity technology 174
  not yet achieved on Earth 39
Aquarius, age of 115, 145
  business model 141
  energies of 127, 143
  new evolutionary stage 141
  private enterprise will still
    exist 142
  qualities of 127
Arab Spring 128
Ariel School, Zimbabwe 26
Arnold, Kenneth 169
Art of Self-realisation 44, 65, 129
Astral planes
  planes of illusion 156
Awareness 53, 115
  prerequisite for change
    129, 130, 146
Axis powers 72

threatens the world 53
Commercials
infringe freedom of thought
52, 63
Communism 75
fall of 128
Competition
corrupts democracy 52
could be replaced by
excellence 63
is divisive 46, 62
must be replaced by
co-operation 114
now accepted as fact of life 65
Consciousness
evolution of 43, 172, 174
expansion of
all major religions share
notion of 135
Consumption
voluntary constraint of 113
Contact from Planet Iarga 38
Contactees
face ridicule 9
messages distorted 143
messages imbued with respect
for human free will 171
messages not escapism 154
Co-operation
and sharing, key to freedom
and justice 115
needs to replace competition
114
Co-operatives 136
Cosmic isolation 7
can be lifted by recognizing
spiritual facts of life 70
self-imposed 68

Cosmic law
against interfering in other
planets 8
Cosmic Science bulletin 4
Cosmos
is vast school 147
Creativity
demonstrates divine origin 151
drives man to do better 140
happiness needed for 112
on 'Iarga' 113
Creme, Benjamin 142-43,
158, 175
on competition 63
on help from Space Brothers
83
says all planets are inhabited
85
says contacts from space
governed by Law 74
says space people cautious
about informing us 6
*The Gathering of the Forces of
Light – UFOs and their
Spiritual Mission* 26
visitors appear as ordinary
humans 9
work with Master of Wisdom
17
Curiosity, Mars rover 23, 24

D

Dark matter
invisible mirror-image of
matter 86
sub-atomic 86
Dawn space probe 24
Day of Declaration 44, 146

on socialism and capitalism
76
use telepathy 158
Materialism
vs spirituality 72
Matthew 146, 167
McDonald, James E
ridiculed unto death 11
US government suppressed
UFO investigation 4
McElroy Jr, Henry 1
Media
do not take extraterrestrial
visits seriously 167
Medvedev, Dimitry 3
Meek, James 51
Menger, Howard 9, 84, 85
describes being taken out of
the body 86
different way of life 4
on telepathy 157
space people are cautious
about informing us 6
UFO cover-up to prevent
economic upset 4
Mercury
Leonardo da Vinci incarnated
from 150
Messiah 43
Mitchell, Dr Edgar 1, 39, 175
Money
not used on other planets
99, 101, 102
Morphogenetic fields
are etheric planes of matter 86
Mutual UFO Network 29
*My Trip to Mars, the Moon and
Venus* 95

N

Nelson, Buck 10, 55, 84, 170
about life on other planets
109
*My Trip to Mars, the Moon and
Venus* 95
Neoliberal policies 48, 52
New Age 115, 145, 148
business model for 141
mystical notion of 127
principle of sharing 92
New world order
history of the term 71
world needs true 73
New World Order, The 73
Nooij, Tineke de 27
*North-South – A Programme for
Survival* 97
North-South division
now in every nation 65
Nuclear weapons 96

O

Obama, Barack 3
State of the Union 2014 47
UFO sighting before
inauguration 17
UFO sighting during
campaign speech 15
'Occupy' 128, 145
Ocean X
Baltic Sea discovery 60
Officials, statements from
are positive disclosure 1
Oneness
humanity's awareness of 127
quality of Aquarius 127

RECOMMENDED READING

HERE TO HELP: UFOs AND THE SPACE BROTHERS

GERARD AARTSEN

Message from space:
Life is One, so live as one
.... or perish

In this book the author reframes the debate about the
intentions of the space visitors in view of the
unprecedented changes engulfing the world today.

BGA Publications, second edition, 2012
Paperback, xii + 187 pages
ISBN: 978-90-815495-3-0

RECOMMENDED READING

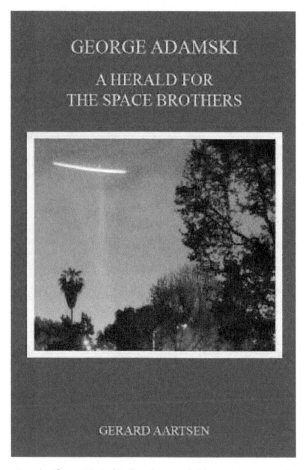

For the first time, this book reveals the true scope of
George Adamski's mission in preparation for a
complete restructuring of our world.

BGA Publications, second edition, 2011
Paperback, xii + 145 pages
ISBN: 978-90-8154-952-3

CPSIA information can be obtained
at www.ICGtesting.com
Printed in the USA
BVOW11s1732220617
487497BV00006B/35/P